# SO YOU WANT TO BE IN MUSICALS?

Ruthie Henshall
with Daniel Bowling

**NICK HERN BOOKS**

London

www.nickhernbooks.co.uk

# A Nick Hern Book

SO YOU WANT TO BE IN MUSICALS?
first published in Great Britain in 2012
by Nick Hern Books Limited,
The Glasshouse, 49a Goldhawk Road, London W12 8QP

Reprinted 2012

Front cover image: © iStockphoto.com/BlackJack3D
Inside front cover photo: Ruthie Henshall as Roxie Hart in
*Chicago*, Adelphi Theatre, London, 1997 © Catherine Ashmore
Inside back cover photo: © Mug Photography
(www.mugphotography.co.uk)
Cover designed by Peter Bennett

Typeset by Nick Hern Books, London
Printed and bound in Great Britain by
Ashford Colour Press, Gosport, Hampshire

A CIP catalogue record for this book
is available from the British Library

ISBN 978 1 84842 150 9

THE UNIVERSITY OF
WINCHESTER

Martial Rose Library
Tel: 01962 827306

To be returned on or before the day marked above, subject to recall.

www.ruthienenshall.com
@RuthieHenshall

# DANIEL BOWLING

Daniel Bowling has served as either music supervisor or music director for many productions in both the UK and US, including *Mary Poppins*, *The Phantom of the Opera*, *Les Misérables*, *Miss Saigon*, *Joseph and the Amazing Technicolor Dreamcoat*, *Jesus Christ Superstar* and *Assassins*. He has had a long association with Andrew Lloyd Webber's *Cats* and has launched productions from Moscow to Madrid.

Over the course of his career, he has auditioned thousands of artists and is the author of *Auditions Undressed*, a guide to taking better auditions (available at danielbowling.co.uk and on Amazon.com). Daniel is a graduate of the Curtis Institute of Music in Philadelphia.

www.danielbowling.co.uk

For my daughters, Lily and Dolly,
And for my mother and father, Gloria and David,
And my sisters, Susan and Abigail.

And in memory of my sister, Noel,
who died in 2007.

*Ruthie*


For my wife, Grainne, and my son, Ciaran,
both of whom continually inspire and unceasingly
support me.

*Daniel*

Our deepest fear is not that we are inadequate. Our deepest fear is that we are powerful beyond measure. It is our light, not our darkness that most frightens us. We ask ourselves, 'Who am I to be brilliant, gorgeous, talented, fabulous?' Actually, who are you not to be? You are a child of God. Your playing small does not serve the world. There is nothing enlightened about shrinking so that other people won't feel insecure around you. We are all meant to shine, as children do. We were born to make manifest the glory of God that is within us. It's not just in some of us; it's in everyone. And as we let our own light shine, we unconsciously give other people permission to do the same. As we are liberated from our own fear, our presence automatically liberates others.

*Marianne Williamson*

# Contents

# Acknowledgements

My thanks to all those people in the theatre who have helped me with this book, some of whom are mentioned or quoted. And my special gratitude goes to Dan Bowling, whose wide-ranging knowledge and experience is spread right through these pages. For most of the time the book was being written, Dan was working in America and I in the UK, which made the task of pulling all the pieces together less than easy. It was done by my journalist father David, who subedited it into shape.

*Ruthie*

A million thanks to Ruthie for writing a book with me whilst on opposite sides of the Atlantic Ocean, and Matt Applewhite at Nick Hern Books for his unending patience and wise counsel.

*Daniel*

# 'Do You Hear the People Sing?'
## Introduction

# Introduction

Do you remember the visceral excitement of being taken to the theatre for the first time? The usher took your ticket as you walked into this amazing place, with its plush red-velvet seats and ornate ceiling, not knowing what you were about to experience or feel. You heard the orchestra warming up and the animated chatter of the audience. Then, the lights dimmed, the overture started and a journey began that transported you in ways you hadn't imagined before. The awakening inside you was stronger than anything you'd ever experienced. The power of the performance changed what you wanted out of life.

My experience on first discovering dancing was as if someone had turned on the brightest light in the world. I loved it and threw myself into it with everything I had. I was lucky because, at the tender age of ten, I had found my passion and I have never for one moment thought of doing anything else. It's arrogant maybe, but there was no doubt in my mind that I wanted to be a 'star'. My sister Noel said to me when I was young that you could have anything you wanted if you wanted it enough – and I wanted this more than enough. I have no doubt that my childhood, which was not without its problems, shaped that desire to be successful.

Every performer I know has had that singular experience – that awakening – in some form or another, either by watching other performers onstage or by starting to do it themselves. In your case, perhaps it came through attending the theatre, or maybe during a moment of childhood play where imagination blossomed into a sort of improvised performance rewarded with a round of applause from your family. Once bitten by the theatrical bug, the potion released almost always persists. Like an itch that can never be scratched enough, that passion for performance just intensifies until you decide to do something about it: to make theatre your life's work. And make no mistake about it: you will have to work. Very hard!

The experience of allowing your imagination to burn brightly, expressing yourself freely and communicating the joy it brings to others, has hopefully brought you to reading this book. There are many books about acting, but no previous 'how-to' guide about the process of getting into musical theatre: training, auditioning, rehearsing, performing and making a career for yourself. The talent contests and 'search for a star' programmes on television have proved there is a lot of untapped talent in Britain. It is to these aspirant professionals – students thinking of going into training and those already there – that this book is aimed. Along the way, we will share some of our own experiences, our top tips and practical advice about the business that we love.

### Why musical theatre?

Why does a story told through the combination of acting, singing and dance resonate particularly with you? Why not simply specialise in one of those three disciplines? Some people are born specialists – they know what they like and they like what they know. The singular focus suits their artistic temperament, but others have a more varied palate and need fuller flavours. Musical theatre is the whole package. As a performer, you get to sing, dance and act for a living; and that can be heaven. But if it's right for you – and you're going to make it work as a career – you must have a real passion for it.

In the show *A Chorus Line*, Morales and the company sing 'What I Did for Love'. In the film, where it's sung by a soloist filled with desire and regret, you might believe it was about romantic love, but that's not its true meaning. The musical was written about a bunch of Broadway gypsies – the New York expression for dancers – auditioning to become the chorus line in a big show. The song is about dancing for the love of it. 'The gift was ours to borrow,' the hopefuls sing, and it really is in many ways.

Nobody stays in musical theatre because it's easy. It takes hard graft to become good at it, just as it does if you want to become a doctor or a lawyer. I trained for more than nine years, and some spend longer, and there is no end to the upkeep of the body and the voice. You have to love what you are doing because the real truth is that you are unlikely to become rich from it. You may get some big jobs, but you will almost certainly also face time out of work – and there will be moments when you despair of ever getting another job.

## Where you should aim

Imagine the costs involved for a producer or director if they discover to their horror that the actor they thought perfect for their starring role can't cope with a basic dance routine or sing an elementary tune. The cost in time and money needed to get somebody the necessary training to complete a simple dance or singing scene can be potentially cata-strophic for those holding the purse strings. When it comes to musical theatre, actors that can't dance, dancers that can't sing, and singers that can't act (or any combination of these) leave themselves limited room for manoeuvre.

In these cash-strapped times, diversity is the name of the game. Extra skills are more and more important – just as they were when the great names made the Metro-Goldwyn-Mayer Studios famous in the 1940s and '50s. They had it all: Judy Garland, Fred Astaire, Gene Kelly, Frank Sinatra, James Stewart, Lucille Ball – I loved their movies and nearly wore out my videotapes through repeat viewing. Producers and directors sought out and employed these 'triple-threat' performers because they got a polished job done with the best use of time and money. Audiences instinctively marvelled at the ease with which these stars negotiated dramatic, choreographed and musical scenes.

Today's competitive industry is just the same. Voice is vital, acting skills essential, and dance indispensible. None of these three skills is totally independent though. You perform a song better if you can act it just as well as you sing it; likewise, you're a more competent actor if your voice has been trained to handle the complex breathing associated with singing. Dancing ability brings a subtlety and ease to all your movement onstage. I doubt if I would have got my breakthrough role in the Gershwin musical *Crazy for You* if I didn't dance.

As primarily a voice coach and musical director, it's interesting that some of the most dramatic transformations that Daniel has witnessed over the years have been through the power of movement or dance: 'It never ceases to amaze me how an actor or singer can intellectualise a scene with little or no progress and yet as soon as they explore it physically or "get it into their bodies", the entire thing sparks off the stage. Similarly, dancers are often so disciplined that until they learn to "let loose" through dramatic improvisation, they often remain theatrically wooden. Singers who can soar with ease through the big ballad "Defying Gravity" from *Wicked* will remain well and truly earthbound if they can't tell the story of the song dramatically or feel physically relaxed and fluid onstage.' The triple talents are not just separate skills to be mastered individually; for a musical-theatre performer they should be indivisible.

It's not always enough being a triple threat any more. There is a growing trend, especially in regional theatre where economy is vital, of staging musicals with actors who possess a 'fourth threat': playing a musical instrument as well. It cuts out the need for an (expensive) separate orchestra, and allows for a (desirable) larger cast, as well as sometimes making a point about the themes of the show. The Watermill Theatre in Newbury, Berkshire, has become a leader in this field, producing John Doyle's actor/musician productions of *Sweeney Todd* and *Mack and Mabel* (which both transferred to the West End). Peter Rowe at the New Wolsey Theatre in Ipswich has had similar successes, including *Guys and Dolls*. In Craig Revel Horwood's production of *Sunset Boulevard*, all the actors played instruments with the exception of Kathryn Evans as Norma Desmond. It's bound to happen more and more – though, of course, not all musicals lend themselves to being performed in this way. It's hard to imagine *Cats* featuring the cast of felines all playing their own instruments. Then again...

## A life in musical theatre

If being a triple threat is what you aspire to – and what you achieve – then what is life as a musical-theatre performer going to give you? Intellectually, you will be endlessly challenged and absorbed. Emotionally, you will enjoy experiences most people only dream of. Physically, you will instill a discipline and care for your body which will, hopefully, grant you a long and healthy life. Creatively, you will be blessed by working with wonderful colleagues who will help you to blossom and evolve. Altruistically, you will give pleasure to more people than you'll ever know and, possibly, actually transform some lives for the better.

Yes, fame and money can follow, but if they take precedence over the less tangible rewards, then the pitfalls of the business can swallow you up and deny you the joys of a unique career. There is no easy way to succeed as a performer, so don't look for quick fixes or shortcuts. They're all a waste of time. Consistent, dedicated work is the only way.

If you are resilient and disciplined enough (and mad enough) to make performing your life, you can travel the world and work in every corner of the business. You will teach and be taught by others and be enriched by it. You will ride a financial roller-coaster whose repeated ups and downs will be interrupted only by frequent stop-offs to see your accountant. You will love and be loved like few others. You will live a life filled with profundity – and you will laugh a lot. Musical theatre will connect you to other people in all sorts of ways, and these connections, with other people in the business or those across the footlights, are what nourish us.

## This book

*So You Want To Be In Musicals?* is obviously aimed at people who answer 'Yes!' to the question posed by that title. Because you're presumably aspiring to reach the very top of the profession (and you've got to aim high if you want to do it at all), we focus on the ultimate goal of a career performing in the West End and on Broadway. Besides, that's our own professional experience, so we can't and don't go into great detail about the many other performing opportunities that are also available. There are many other books that cover those.

We aim to show you where you need to develop your abilities, and the decisions and choices you will have to make along the way. We don't try to teach you those skills that you will have to acquire for yourself through training, hard graft and perseverance. A book can't teach you time steps or how to belt in the first place, so it takes it as read that you already have the talent, or the potential to develop it.

Building that talent and learning everything you can about the business is paramount, and getting that first job is what it's all about – and then where you go next. Good fortune will certainly play a part in your career, as it does in all our lives, but you can always give luck a nudge. We hope this book will give you the nudge – and the edge – you need.

*Ruthie Henshall and Daniel Bowling*

# 'I'd Do Anything'
# Part One: Training

# 1

# Training

The sociologist and author Malcolm Gladwell suggested that you need to spend ten thousand hours training and practising your skills before you can even think of achieving command over your chosen field. That's quite a bit more than working every single hour for a whole year. So, given that you can't train non-stop, you're talking about a long time to achieve that target. According to Gladwell, intelligence, talent, opportunity and luck all have far less to do with ultimate success than the unglamorous truth that hard work over a long period is actually what results in mastery and eventual prosperity.

Gladwell cites many examples of great musicians, artists, scientists, inventors and athletes who only emerge as the top dog at what they do after devoting at least three hours a day to it for a decade. So, if you want to win Wimbledon at the age of seventeen, like Boris Becker, you need to hammer tennis balls about for at least 180 minutes a day from the age of six. One of the world's greatest violinists, Maxim Vengerov, was taught by his mother. Lessons started after dinner and continued until four in the morning – when he was just four years old! He said, 'It was torture. But I became a violinist within two years.' He won his first international prize at the age of fifteen. Michael Jackson was hailed as an overnight prodigy by *Rolling Stone* magazine when he was ten years old. But Michael had joined his brother's band when he was six, and so had already spent four years rehearsing and performing.

We have a tendency to think that the Beckers, Vengerovs and Jacksons of this world are lucky and blessed with a rare talent, phenomenal gifts that hand them their brilliance without much effort. But the reality is that these people have given over long stretches of their lives, sacrificing everyday pleasures, to achieve their extraordinary level of brilliance and success.

I'm not for one moment suggesting that it is a good idea to cram thousands of hours of training into four years at the age of six. Sadly, we know how that story ended for Michael Jackson. But when all that work takes place over a healthier time span, remarkable results can occur. Put simply, the people who put in the practice make their own luck. The notion of an 'overnight success' really doesn't exist. You always have to graft for it. Without this, mastery of your craft may well elude you.

Ten thousand hours sounds like a long and unachievable amount of time. Don't get too hung up on it; it's a fairly arbitrary figure and one man's opinion. But the message behind it makes a lot of sense. If you think that the average person in Britain watches more than four hours of television a day – twenty-eight hours a week, 1,456 hours a year – it puts the whole business into some sort of reasonable, achievable perspective. At that rate, it would take seven years for the average person to watch television for ten thousand hours. It doesn't mean you've got to toss your TV on the scrapheap, but it should almost certainly play a smaller part in your life if you want to be the best. Today, if your favourite programmes clash with your training, they are easily recorded digitally or can be viewed online at a more convenient moment. This is the way top achievers think – the athletes who win Olympic gold medals or anyone who achieves great success – and it's a good idea to get used to it anyway because, if you make it in musical theatre, your nights as a couch potato will be much reduced.

Back in the nineteenth century, the writer Henry David Thoreau said, 'Go confidently in the direction of your dreams.

Live the life you have imagined.' It's a lovely quote for people in our business because so many of us are driven by a dream; but we need to understand that to 'go confidently' in musical theatre will require a colossal amount of hard work, sweat and, probably, more than a few tears too. You will also require the assistance of other people around you. Practically, no one makes it without a great deal of help and how you choose those to support you can be an important factor in your ultimate success, artistically and professionally.

The ways into musical theatre are fairly limited: drama schools and university courses (which can also offer a useful teaching qualification) or, once in a while, there's the chance that someone will get spotted in an amateur production or discovered and taken on by a talent agency. But, ideally, you should be convinced of the merits of pursuing a full, multi-faceted training, which prepares people in the way no other single route can. Of course, each student will have their own individual strengths, but musical-theatre training insists that each student has a strong and reliable technique in all three branches of the performing arts: acting, singing and dancing. We have to be aware that producers and directors in all aspects of the business are turning more and more to artists with this specialist training and skills.

This chapter begins by considering the range of opportunities available as you start to look ahead to your career, how to maximise your chances of getting a place on a training course, and what to concentrate on – and how to conduct yourself – once you have.

## School

Some people know they want a career in musical theatre from a very young age – and there are specialist schools that can offer this sort of training, sometimes coming with some form of scholarship. However, most aspiring performers won't go to these sorts of stage schools, and it can be frustrating to be stuck in a school classroom, memorising capital cities or calculating square roots, when they are really dreaming about taking a dance class or a singing lesson instead. As we well know, the academic pressures just mount with each successive term of education, particularly in the build-up to examinations in the later years. So it's important that you jump through the necessary academic hoops, even if you're set on a career on the stage. You may not be clamouring to know the largest city in Illinois or the square root of eighty-one, but a lot of what you learn will be vital, one way or another.

What we learn in school goes far beyond just tucking away facts and figures. We progress and mature as people, discover how to research and gather information, and become more disciplined workers from completing all manner of tasks. We grow in independence and confidence by tackling new challenges, and we grasp processes that ultimately help us succeed in both our professional and private lives. Work that falls outside your real passion is *never* a waste of time, because it helps to build the mindset that is essential to achieve success in any career, including musical theatre.

If you're currently still at school, make the most of all opportunities (especially in school drama productions), use every possible resource on offer and assimilate everything you can – not for the grades or the teaching staff, but because you will need an attitude of working hard and strong personal discipline to make it in musical theatre. It will serve as a firm foundation for all those exhausting hours of practice you will face to build a career in a very tough business.

Schools like pupils who get A grades in their exams, but they also love those who do well in the theatre. I absolutely guarantee that when you're starring in the West End or on Broadway, they'll be the first to laud your success and invite you back to speak at their next awards ceremony.

It's not only academic hurdles we've got to jump; there are sometimes parental ones as well. Ironically, in my case, it was actually my primary-school headmistress who approached my father and suggested sending me to a theatre school. She was keenly aware of my passion for performing – and, as a good old-fashioned educationist, she said it was a recommendation she had never considered making before. But my father said no, and I was heartbroken. He said that I should continue a formal education because I might change my mind. But he added that if I still felt the same when I was sixteen, then he would do everything in his power to help me into drama school. And that's what happened. Encouraged also by my ballet and dance teacher, Mrs Sams, and my dance teacher at Bullers Wood School in Chislehurst, the aptly named Mrs Tapp, I auditioned for Laine Theatre Arts in Epsom, and got a place. It was a terrific training, but not all those who graduated with me made it into musical theatre. Some found it too hot for them and went into teaching or off in different directions, but most wouldn't have missed it for the world.

Even if a specialist stage school is not an option for you, then hopefully there will be opportunities to be involved in drama and music at your school. There are several academic qualifications that may be on the syllabus: A levels (or Highers in Scotland) in Theatre Studies, BTEC courses in Performing Arts, and so on. If these are not on offer, then seek training outside. Stay focused and enthusiastic, and find the best teachers you can to help you pursue your ambitions.

## Outside School

### Youth theatres

If you're between the ages of twelve and eighteen – or often even younger – there are organisations that provide outstanding opportunities to learn and perform. In the UK, two of the most prestigious ones providing top-level training outside of a school environment are the National Youth Theatre and the National Youth Music Theatre. Over the years, hundreds of West End performers have got their start with one of them. There are countless other smaller youth theatres – on a regional, county and local level.

- The National Youth Theatre (NYT) offers a series of acting courses for students, emphasising ensemble playing, devised work and improvisation. The courses usually last a couple of weeks, where up to thirty students create and perform under the guidance of a professional director. In addition to the acting courses, the company also offers technical courses for new and existing members to gain practical training and experience in lighting and sound, stage management, costume, scenery and props. Every year the company puts on several productions, around the UK and sometimes beyond, cast from members who have done the courses.

- The National Youth Music Theatre (NYMT) operates in a similar way, but obviously with an emphasis on musical theatre. The company explores new and existing works, inspires young people and gives them the opportunity to expand their talent, imagination and creativity. Both NYT and NYMT are very competitive; they receive over four thousand applicants each year for only a few hundred new places. If you apply to either organisation, you are guaranteed an audition, which is excellent experience. Part Two of this book explores how you can best prepare for an audition.

- The National Association of Youth Theatres is the development agency supporting youth theatres in England, and another great resource to explore the opportunities to train and perform. Founded in 1982, NAYT works with over a thousand groups and individuals to support the development of youth-theatre activity.

- Youth Music Theatre UK was founded in 2003 and is the UK's biggest provider of music-theatre projects for young people. At the core of YMT's activity are its residential projects, which usually take place during the summer. Young people from around the country audition for eight new pieces of musical theatre that are then developed, rehearsed and staged in professional theatres. The young people have a hand in creating and devising original pieces, supported by theatre professionals. The company also runs non-audition courses, called The Studio, and operates a successful outreach programme, working with young people from disadvantaged backgrounds. All of the company's projects are specially commissioned and often developed over two or more summers.

- Youth Dance England (YDE) is obviously aimed at those primarily interested in dance. The organisation's aim is to increase dance opportunities for all children and young people on a national scale, both in and out of school settings, and is a great resource for finding the best training near you.

## Classes and coaching

Virtually every city and large town in Britain will have private performing-arts schools or academies, or individual tutors offering classes or training in singing, dancing or acting. They can be a good place to begin to find the level of training you'll need to make it in the business. Some accept students quite young and if you're serious about musical theatre, you need to start as early as possible.

Ideally, you will get singing lessons, join a dance class (preferably in more than one discipline – ballet, jazz and tap), and receive acting tuition. There are franchise organisations such as Stagecoach, Razzamataz and Theatretrain who offer weekend classes for younger students. Many performing-arts colleges and drama schools offer short, part-time courses, often during the summer months when their regular students are on vacation. These summer schools are a useful introduction to the rigours of a full training course and a good insight into what the business is all about and what it will want from you.

Generally under the tuition of a private coach, you can study and prepare for examinations in each different field, administered and awarded by organisations like the Royal Academies of Music or Dance, LAMDA, Trinity College and Guildhall. Examinations can be an excellent addition to your CV, and give you a very definite sense of progress as you acquire new skills and move up the grades. But it doesn't come cheap. Teachers at your school may be able to suggest less costly ways of getting the training you need – or, possibly, be able to offer tuition themselves. Don't be afraid to ask; our profession calls for courage. And don't forget to check for scholarship places. They are available in all sorts of places now for young people with a notable talent. *The Stage*, the weekly bible of the entertainment business, has an excellent training section that gives up-to-date details of the many opportunities available, and is also involved in providing scholarships to various drama schools.

*Amateur theatre*

There are other cost-effective ways of practising your skills. Joining a local choir is a great way to develop your voice, improve your musicality, and get used to singing regularly. There is the useful performance element too, and it can be great fun being part of a group dedicated to learning, staging and harmonising songs. Many professional performers began by treading the boards with their local amateur theatre company, and it is still one of the best ways to develop your skills and fulfil your love of performing.

The quality of amateur theatre varies wildly, and many of the participants will be involved principally to have a good time – and there's nothing wrong with that. But larger towns and cities will probably have several very competent amateur companies, filled with dedicated performers and creative people, who put on large-scale shows, often musicals, for a week or so in local theatres. A lot of these productions get very close to professional standards – and very occasionally better – so it's definitely worth joining a good amateur group. It's an unrivalled chance to play some of the wonderful roles in the musical-theatre repertoire. There are three major organisations representing amateur theatre in the UK that can help you find your most appropriate local group:

- The National Operatic and Dramatic Association (NODA) was founded in 1899, and has a membership of around 2,400 amateur theatre companies throughout the United Kingdom. These wide-ranging societies stage musicals, operas, plays, concerts and pantomimes in a variety of venues, ranging from professional theatres that the companies hire to village halls.

- The Little Theatre Guild of Great Britain (LTG), founded in 1946, represents amateur companies which are generally larger and control their own premises. It has 103 members located in England, and boasts Sir Ian McKellen as a Patron. He has said: 'Like many professional actors, I am a graduate of the Little Theatre Guild, whose member theatres are spread across the country.'

- The National Drama Festivals Association caters for amateur theatre groups that participate in local drama festivals. There are over one hundred such festivals of one-act and full-length productions, involving in excess of five hundred amateur theatre companies.

*Personal time*

Involvement in any of these amateur organisations – and the opportunities they offer – will show you if a life in musicals is really what you want. The other vital thing in your early preparation for a career in musical theatre is to learn as much about the form as you can. There are books on the subject, but it's particularly useful to listen to the classic musical scores and watch the great films. Just singing along to a Sondheim soundtrack in your bedroom is valuable practice that moves you towards your goal.

You can never know too much about the exciting business you want to be part of. One agent summed up to me what students have to do: 'They've got to live it, eat it, and sleep it – even the history. You'd be amazed how many students don't seem to have heard of Gene Kelly.' Use your student card and get to see as many plays and shows as you can. A lot of theatres do student rates and sell off good seats cheaply shortly before curtain-up. It may mean standing in line for a bit, but it's worth it. Watch and learn. Not every performer and every show will do it for you, but you will learn valuable lessons about performing by watching all forms and styles of performance. The aim of all this is that you improve your knowledge and experiences as you move on to that next stage in your training: drama school.

## Applying to Drama School

*Choosing the school*

When choosing your training course, you need to think about who you are, exactly what you want to become, and how you're going to achieve it. You need to start your research early and become aware of the different options available to you (there is a list in the Appendix of the opportunities currently in the UK). Here are some suggestions for when you're researching different courses and schools:

- Visit Drama UK (formerly the Conference of Drama Schools and the National Council for Drama Training), the umbrella organisation for the top drama schools in the UK, for further listings and tips on the timetable of applying.

- Read the prospectuses of all the schools; you can send off for them or read them online. Get a sense of the school's strengths, the average timetable, how many hours a week you'll get training (it should be around thirty), the size of classes and the quality of the facilities.

- Visit the schools that interest you at open days or, if you can, attend their final-year productions to give you a sense of the students at work.

- Talk to staff to get a sense of their personalities, spirit and areas of interest; and talk to current and recently graduated students for a reasonably unbiased view.

I know getting into a drama school can be tough enough anyway, but don't sell yourself short. If you want to succeed in this business, you should make every effort to search out the best training ground for your needs. Making the decision based on other reasons ('My singing teacher recommended it', 'My best friend went there', 'It's close to where I live' and so on) may work out fine in the end, but you might easily be missing something better. All of us who reach for the stars have to believe that we're going to make it, regardless of where we train. But the smart ones try to load the dice in their favour as much as they can.

My first love was for dancing; my passion for singing came later; and my desire to act after that. As a late starter at ten years old, I saw myself as a natural partner for Rudolf Nureyev and was so keen that I never missed a single ballet class. But my teacher was aware from quite early on that, although I was reasonably talented, I was never destined for the Royal Ballet. I had to accept later that I was the wrong body type and needed to concentrate on building up other skills. You have to be self-aware enough to acknowledge your strengths *and* your weaknesses, and the sort of career you should realistically aim for. My years of ballet were not wasted. I certainly needed it when I played Maggie in *A Chorus Line*, and the point work came in useful when, with Julia McKenzie and Bernadette Peters, I performed Sondheim's 'You've Gotta Have a Gimmick' in *Hey, Mr Producer!* (the great concert celebration of Sir Cameron Mackintosh's musicals; my family have worn out that part of the videotape!).

## Making your application

On a practical level, every drama school or university course will have different criteria for entry. It's your job to find out what those requirements are and know what you must achieve to be offered a place or, even better, a scholarship. Your job is to knuckle down and reach the level of ability necessary to win your place. You won't do it without the legwork.

Most drama-school websites today feature information about dates and fees, and you should be able to investigate any relevant information, as well as download the appropriate application forms. Additionally, they will list their open days. Typically, these take place in September and October the year before you would actually attend, which gives you good time to prepare your shortlist of schools.

Most schools require you to submit an application usually no later than mid-January to be guaranteed an audition for courses that begin later that year, but many schools start to accept applications for entry twelve months in advance. It is generally advisable to apply as early as is consistent with having made a careful and considered choice of institutions and training courses. Be careful not to leave it too late.

Don't assume that every school adheres to a similar timetable for application deadlines and audition dates. Mark clearly in your diary the ones you are planning to apply to – and remember that each school may have different audition criteria, which can mean you end up preparing much more material than you had initially planned for. Get organised and give yourself the maximum amount of time to have your audition ready. Nothing worth achieving is ever easy, but sensible, sound preparation will make the process not only less painful but possibly even enjoyable.

You will generally have to pay to cover the costs of your audition at each school. So, adding in travelling expenses and maybe overnight accommodation, you need to pick carefully and limit the number of schools to a realistic number. Putting all your eggs in one basket is not recommended, however. You should only apply to schools where you'd genuinely consider going.

## Preparing for auditions

As already mentioned, each one of your shortlisted schools will have different audition requirements, but it's important to anticipate what is typical or the norm, so you can judge and prepare for those aspects of the process that are likely to be consistent. Drama schools are obliged to provide candidates with all relevant information before and during the selection process. The audition/interview procedure should be clearly outlined in advance, telling you how, where and when it will take place. Especially important is any detailed information of how that particular school assesses candidates. This information should be the foundation of how you equip yourself for the audition.

Drama schools will be assessing your abilities in the three musical-theatre disciplines – acting, singing and dancing. Potential is judged by an expert panel and the strongest candidates will usually be given a recall audition and will be serious contenders for places on the course. You will need to excel in at least one of the three disciplines and have a good underpinning of the other two. Where candidates have particular difficulties outside of their principle discipline, ultimately it is up to each audition panel to determine whether or not they can accommodate or redress these shortcomings. Try not to put yourself in that position. However good you feel you are, you could be limiting your chances if you focus on just one of the disciplines in preparation for your audition. Competence in all three is likely to increase your prospects of acceptance and get you a career in musical theatre. That said, no school is going to turn its back on brilliance.

Audition panels will usually consist of at least two members who will be professional actors, directors, musical directors, casting directors or course directors of the school's faculty. If this is not detailed in the information provided, feel free to ask. It's extremely important that those who are hearing your audition represent some sort of cross-section of experience so that dialogue and debate is built into the system. All schools endeavour to make the audition process as fair and smooth as possible, but arming yourself with as much information and knowledge of their specific criteria and perhaps their attitude toward the audition itself, can take some of the anxiety out of the process, as well as maybe enabling you to remain flexible should things take an unexpected turn.

The audition panel has to make informed choices about potential students and their ability to undertake the type of tough training that a musical-theatre course will require. They will be looking for physical energy, an active mind, good health, the ability to use your imagination and transform written text through song and speech into theatrically believable words and thought. Typically, two contrasting songs are compulsory. Have your sheet music prepared with clear cuts and directions for the pianist. Monologues from plays are usually required – they should be no longer than two minutes and you may be asked for something classical, usually Shakespeare. Some schools will provide you with lists of speeches they want you to choose from. Always be prepared to listen to any direction that you may be offered by the panel, and be malleable enough to respond to it. Your dance or movement experience will be explored, perhaps in a class or session with other candidates, and an interview will very likely take place as well.

Choose material that is appropriate to you and your strengths – and the drama school where you are applying. When you choose audition pieces that fit you like a glove, it not only enables you to connect with the song or mono-logue more intuitively, but it really tells those judging that you've done your homework, know who you are and have good idea where you're going as an artist. Part Two of this book looks in more detail at the process of auditioning, including choosing and preparing your pieces.

## Going to Drama School

Let's assume that you've won that much-coveted place at the school of your choice (well done!), on a typical three-year undergraduate training in musical theatre that will take you to a high degree of proficiency in acting, singing and danc-ing. Equal emphasis will be placed on each of these three disciplines in order to produce rounded performers with all the necessary accomplishments. Schools want success – for the students and, naturally, for their own reputations as well.

After the initial excitement of starting your new course and meeting your tutors and fellow classmates, you will begin to work on the techniques you'll need to sustain a career as a professional performer. First-year acting classes are likely to focus on improvisation and developing your imagination; understanding who you are so you can begin to explore other characters and personalities; listening and reacting spontaneously and truthfully in inventive situations. Weekly practical singing classes, small group repertoire classes, and one-to-one tutorials are usually standard for developing your voice and, importantly, your breathing. You will have dance classes in tap, ballet, jazz and contemporary, as well as a variety of other movement and fitness classes.

Your second year should be about the consolidation of these techniques but with greater diversity and exposure to other specialised styles, tutors and directors. You can expect song preparation and presentation, workshops, masterclasses and performance opportunities to feature more frequently as you work to fuse the acting, singing and dancing together. Third-year classes will fortify your understanding of professional practice, and prepare you for the big workplace battle ahead. There'll be quite a lot of performance as well as audition preparation and technique. Special projects are often introduced, full-scale musicals rehearsed and staged, along with agent showcases. All in all, it's an exciting, exhilarating, exhausting time ahead of you.

*The costs*

Everything has a cost – and training in musical theatre is no exception. Fees vary dramatically, so this business requires a relentless spirit and an economically creative mind. The sooner you begin to think resourcefully when it comes to money, the better. Students who have paid their own way through training – perhaps with a combination of scholarships, grants, teaching, apprenticeships and part-time jobs – are often the ones who will ultimately succeed. Their ingenuity and innovation will have already given them many of the right tools to sustain a career in the performing arts. Knowing how to grapple with a bit of hard graft will hold you in good stead for when you graduate and enter the profession. Your school should be able to give you advice on what loans, grants and scholarships are available to you, and Drama UK offers valuable advice and support. Speaking to other students about how they survived financially can also be useful.

When I started training, I was lucky enough to get a grant – but this was reduced sharply later, and I was forced to take an evening job as a kitchen assistant in a restaurant, then as a waitress and finally as bar staff. The money was good, but the temptation to party was also there. I succumbed a few times and suffered the morning after, but quickly realised that this was a pointless waste of time, energy – and money I hadn't got. Like other West End performers, today I receive a host of heartbreaking letters from students asking me to help them financially. I would have to be a multimillionaire or a philanthropic, bonus-rich banker to be of real use, but I tell them all that the most purposeful, resolute and unwavering of them will make it somehow. That is something I have to believe – it would be too sad to think otherwise.

The financial cost of training pales in comparison to how a life in musical theatre will often drain you emotionally and physically. Your body will very likely endure every imaginable punishment over time, and unless you start now to prepare yourself physically as if you were a competitive athlete, you are already limiting your career chances.

Emotional costs are harder to quantify because we all want different things in our personal lives, but maintaining relationships with partners and family will often be stretched to the limit because of your passion to become a performer. Your work can carry you far away from home and for long periods. In some instances, those human connections will be made stronger because of the challenges you face in pursuing your dream, but there are sometimes casualties along the way and that is something you should keep in mind.

## Your Attitude for Training

### Enthusiasm

Your professional reputation is being formed as soon as you start training, whether you recognise it or not. A willingness to learn and conducting yourself with pride will help you cultivate a name people can remember and admire. I enjoyed every moment of my time at Laine Theatre Arts (though I wasn't always the perfect student, as Betty Laine sometimes reminds me!), and I quickly found a way of buckling down and gaining knowledge from every class and every teacher. In fact, there's nobody from whom you can't learn something, even your classmates.

One or two of the friendships you make during your training will very likely last a lifetime, so stay open to the opportunities on offer and the people you meet. Keeping constantly on your toes will help you to forge a good relationship with your peers, and the school. Genuine enthusiasm has the magical ability to lift every aspect of your student life and, when an actor has this passion, people listen and respond better, they relax and frequently perform more freely. One lecturer told me that enthusiastic students are contagious and seem to infect the entire school with their optimism.

### Strength and self-respect

The opposite of this optimism is negativity. Keep your personal problems or bad temper to yourself. Little spats, bubbling on the end of nerves and anxiety, will spark occasionally in a tense theatrical atmosphere, but if you build a troublesome reputation, it can lose you a lot more than friends. I have known talented performers who have virtually disappeared from the business quite early in their careers because of this sort of thing.

Coping with the tricky emotions surrounding fierce competition, criticism and rejection is particularly difficult in the arts because our performances are intimately linked to our sense of self-worth, especially when we are students. Some of us struggle to find objectivity when our portrayals are taken to task, but this is something we have all got to learn to cope with in the fullness of time. We also have to come to terms with the feeling that somebody else has got the part that we feel so strongly we are far better suited to – something I have felt more often than I really care to admit.

This will happen at school as well – the song you absolutely know should really be yours, or the dance you are certain you can do so much better than the person who's got it. It's all painful, occasionally unfair, but it is part of life in theatre and something you are going to have to learn to live with. That's not to say you shouldn't at least tell your teachers how you feel about these things, especially if you feel you are being unjustly overlooked for some reason.

Tutors would be extremely remiss not to prepare you for the realities of this fiercely competitive business, but how they do it is the question. If you think at any stage your confidence and self-worth is being undermined, you have the right to complain. The vast majority of teachers will have your real interests at heart. They too are looking for the best, but they are also human and can make mistakes. However, it's vital that you begin to discover the objectivity and strength necessary to survive in this tough old life. As a young performer, you must try to put in place a method of dealing with the inevitable brickbats and disappointments, as well as the joys of success that musical theatre is likely to bring.

## Connections

Good teachers are impassioned and obsessive about their subject, with an infectious curiosity about all aspects of their art. They understand the courage required to take an audition, the discipline needed to refine a good technique, the mystery and art in giving a great performance. They will work with each student in an entirely unique way, recognising and respecting their individuality and originality. The best will ask the tough questions and continually dare you to be better, helping you find ways to relax and make your work look effortless. Identify the good teachers, respect them, and devour all the knowledge and expertise you possibly can from them.

## Your Health and Well-being

### Your body

We're told that beauty is in the eye of the beholder, which means, of course, that different beholders have very different ideas about what is physically appealing – and that's great. Nevertheless, students are often painfully aware that body shape and image will frequently play a deciding factor in musical-theatre careers. However persuasive your talent and skill may be, we know that what you look like – specifically, your attractiveness to a broad range of people – will often be an additional consideration when the parts are up for grabs. This may be disheartening, even offensive to some, but the truth is, as Daniel puts it, 'that audiences have a tendency to choose sex over substance, and every director knows it'.

You may feel unhappy with your body shape at drama school, or throughout your career. There may be a lot of tall, slim, attractive girls or fit, muscular boys around, and perhaps you feel overweight or underdeveloped alongside them. Everyone is different and not always the 'perfect' shape, but the business tends to make room for us all, and I think the most vital consideration is making sure you are healthy. If you want to get certain roles, then you are going to have to watch what you eat, or go to the gym more regularly. I had a battle to keep my weight down when I was at drama school, because I worked at McDonald's three evenings a week and could eat what I liked during breaks. During both my pregnancies I put on a great deal of extra 'timber'. After my first baby, I was twenty-one pounds heavier than before, but being in a demanding show (and on the '*Chicago* Dance Diet') soon got rid of that. After the second pregnancy, however, I needed Weight Watchers to help me lose twenty-three pounds.

Never crash-diet. All that happens is that your body suffers from food deprivation, it stores practically everything and anything you do eat, and can sap your energy and concentration. There's a lot of truth in the old adages of 'Everything in moderation' and 'A little of what you fancy does you good'. Smaller portions and just a few treats can go a long way in the battle of the bulge.

The other danger is that crash-dieting can lead to anorexia. Don't go down that route. It's dangerous and imprisons people in its life-threatening thrall. Eating disorders are not the sole domain of girls. There are an increasing number of boys affected by both anorexia and bulimia. There is often a link between male eating disorders and athletic prowess, and the quest for physical perfection can result in damaging behaviour associated with diet, supplements and exercise. The use of steroids among young men is on the rise. In a society that places so much value on body image, they are unfortunately seen as a quick and easy response to that pressure. There are many bad side effects, including liver damage, sexual difficulties, aggressive behaviour, depression, acne, muscle spasms and interference with normal growth. If you can't get the body you want with normal exercise, don't take risks.

Ultimately, health is the core to beauty and a good appearance – and your health is one thing you can really control. Exercise, diet and attitude will improve skin, weight, muscle tone, vitality, confidence and even glamour. Perhaps the day will come when you'll want to get your teeth whitened, but if you are physically on top form, whatever minor physical imperfections you think you possess will worry you less and, consequently, be less obvious to anyone else. We are not all meant or able to be thin or muscled or whatever, so learning to accept the body you have is an important lesson.

## Your mind

Your mental health is intertwined with your physical health. Each has a profound effect on the other, and both need to be strengthened and rested in equal measure. In many ways, your mental health is at its most vulnerable as a student; especially, I feel, as a performing-arts student. The courses are tough and demanding, and once in a while it's a great idea to clear your mind, turn your mobile phone off and relax. I have various ways of doing this: having a bath and listening to a piece of music; long vigorous walks or simply lying on my back and concentrating on my breathing. Occasionally I run or ride my bike, and once in a while I fancy a long, hot luxurious sauna. Just doing something simple every so often is a marvellous way of sweeping away any cobwebs and the stress of work.

If we make time to switch off and shut down, when we turn back on, we can do what we do so much better. Sustaining your enthusiasm and optimism is so much easier when occasionally you give yourself the space and time to breathe. Breaking routines, learning new things, drifting, experimenting are essential parts of happiness. You have a life crammed with activity but try to find time to recharge the creative batteries.

## Alcohol and drugs

As a student you are preparing yourself not just for your career but also for the adult world. Experimenting will be part of that, as will be having a drink – as long as it's in moderation. But stay away from drugs. They give you the feeling that you are fabulous and that you can do anything. I promise you that if you saw yourself on playback the following morning, the embarrassment would almost certainly stop you doing it again. People claim that marijuana (dope, hash, whatever name you want to give it) is harmless, but we now know categorically that regular use can lead to forms of psychosis. There are people who suffer from schizophrenia as a direct result of using hash from an early age, and I know this to be true because it happened to a young man known to my family. This poor guy is a mental wreck, his life totally lost, spending most of his time in specialist care. I've never met anybody who is a better performer or a nicer person from taking drugs. They can also kill, and frequently do. Drink can be just as dangerous if you let it take hold and it has ended more theatre careers than you can ever imagine.

## Leaving Drama School

Part Five of this book is dedicated to what happens after you leave drama school and how to develop your career. I expect your school will guide you through this transition too, because it can be an emotional, difficult time. The window of opportunity in which you have to make your mark is not all that big, so you're going to have to make the most of it. You have been studying and training in some sort of educational institution for as long as you can remember and now you are joining a fiercely competitive world without the close support or safety net of the school environment.

Fortunately, you're not alone: there's the rest of the graduates from your school, some of whom will be close friends.

Keep those relationships going; they will enrich and sustain you for the battle ahead – and it *will* be a battle because you are also joining the workplace with all the other newly graduating students from drama schools all over the country. They are your rivals and now you must find ways to shine brighter than they do. During your training you will have developed your own performance style, built certain strengths and smoothed out the weaknesses. But training is only the start (and indeed you never stop learning and developing throughout your career). Now comes the exciting opportunity to put into practice everything you've learnt – everything you've become – up to this point.

## Other Options

Going to drama school is by no means the only training option. Successful performers do come from a university background, others from summer schools or short courses and, every so often, somebody gets in more or less directly from amateur theatre. If you've got what it takes and can find a way of spreading it around, the chances are the business will pick it up. But clearly a full three-year training is the most desirable, most productive option, and the one most likely to bring you eventual success.

The top West End agents I have spoken to make no bones about the fact that most of the new clients they represent have come from a drama-school training. But they also recognise there's still a lot of undiscovered talent out there, trained or otherwise – as recent casting shows on television have made very clear. To date, these contests have generally been won by professionals in the early stages of their careers, sometimes with a full training just behind them and waiting for that first big break. David Grindrod, the leading casting director involved in many of these series, says that drama-school graduates were initially hesitant about coming forward to audition for a televised casting process, 'but once they saw what the prize was, they came in droves. Hopefully we can help some of them on their way. We gave them a hook, and a chance to be a star. The programmes will have given more people the opportunity to feel they can do it.'

Certainly, Danielle Hope had no formal training when she won *Over the Rainbow*, Andrew Lloyd Webber's search for a new Dorothy for his production of *The Wizard of Oz*. A life in musical theatre is not for the faint-hearted, though. Eight shows a week is a tough gig. David Grindrod confirms that 'it's best to get a training. It's like the Olympics – you've got to have that stamina and training to fall back on, especially when you don't feel well. We always tell people to go and get trained if they possibly can.' So that's exactly what Danielle Hope did. Between winning the show and starting rehearsals to play Dorothy, she was sent on a three-month intensive course. There's really no alternative. You need to combine your talent and passion with the proper technique and hard graft that comes from a proper musical-theatre training.

'I Hope I Get It'
Part Two: Auditioning

## 2

# Auditioning

Auditions provide the opportunity for you to show the teaching staff of a drama school or the artistic team of a production what you can do, and you'll have a hard time achieving that if you're standing in the back with your hands in your pockets, as it were. Not stepping up to the front and doing everything in your power to strut your stuff is the equivalent of sending out letters and CVs to potential employers, but leaving off your name and address.

We live in a fiercely competitive world and auditions are the best chance for you to create an impression. Of course, there is always a fine line between confidence and conceit – and we're not suggesting you spend all your time trying to show the world how good you are – but an audition offers the moment to shine. Be ready to take it.

You must have a realistic view about the role auditions play in your career if you are to stay enthusiastic and positive. By the end of each process, countless good performers will have taken part, but only a few, perhaps just one, will have been chosen. They will often have succeeded not necessarily because they were better than everyone else, but simply because, on this occasion, they fit the role best. The needs of the creative team must ultimately serve the production, not any egos those auditioning may have. The reality is that in any selection system, many very talented artists won't get the job.

## A learning experience

Looked at positively, every audition teaches you something – whether you get the job or not. I had my first lesson at the age of ten, trying to be cast in a revival of *Annie*. I joined the long queue of hopefuls stretching from the stage door of the Victoria Palace Theatre right round the block. There was a heaving crocodile of little girls with their mothers in tow, singing, hopping and tapping impatiently along the pavement.

It was hours before I finally reached the front of the queue, certain that I was perfect for the title role. Full of excitement, I leapt through the stage door where a woman summarily measured me, declared me half an inch too tall and sent me packing. The streets around the theatre were a wasteland of devastated dreams for a great many little girls that day, and I was no exception; I sobbed all the way home. But that audition became my first essential lesson in understanding that showbusiness knows what it's looking for and is ruthless in the pursuit of what it sees as perfection. If you're not the right height, sometimes you won't even get through the door.

For some, the inglorious experience of being turned down spells the end of the road, the dread of experiencing that disappointment outweighing any future desire to perform. But those who chase the ambition of being in musicals have to overcome any fear of rejection. It's vital to turn every audition into an opportunity to learn something new. Focus on the positives, reinforce what went right, and look forward to the next one. Auditions should never become mortifying or wretched experiences. You must equate them with opportunity. *Carpe diem* – seize the day and shine.

## The audition panel

Before we talk about preparing for an audition, it's important to consider what it actually hopes to achieve. It is the opportunity for performers to show a creative team (director, producer, casting director, choreographer, musical director, whoever) their potential to take on a specific role or roles in a specific show. Unlike television talent shows, where entertaining the audience at home can take precedence over finding artists with real talent and substance, auditions are not held to embarrass or humiliate performers. They are not aimed at exposing your weaknesses or revealing your secret fears; they are just the theatre world's equivalent of a job interview. The people conducting them want to find the best person for a particular job, nothing more, nothing less. In musical theatre, no director, musical director or choreographer is interested in stripping away your self-worth or dignity. Quite the contrary. You'll find most audition panels mumbling a prayer that you'll be the one who has just what they're looking for. It's in their best interests to be supportive and helpful, so they can truly see what you've got to offer.

When I had the opportunity to sit in on auditions for *A Chorus Line* in New York, I was impressed by the consideration shown to the singers and dancers (much more than is shown to the fictional dancers in the musical itself!). The panel were anxious for each auditionee to show what they could really do, because it would make their job that much easier. They watched and listened with great attentiveness and patience. They were encouraging and asked interested questions. And the moment they saw something they liked, they said so. Often, those who were praised for doing something good got a recall and, even if they didn't, they left with their heads held high, feeling better for the comments they received. Always remember, these people are on your side.

Having said that, you can never second-guess what the auditioners are thinking. Sometimes you'll feel a job is yours, in the bag, and it isn't. Sometimes you'll think you've lost it, only to find you've got it after all. I vividly remember sitting in my car in a traffic jam on London's King's Road after my fifth audition for *Crazy for You*. I wanted to play Polly more than anything, but had no idea how I stood in the eyes of the creative team and producers. Told nothing by any of them, the stress and frustration had me sobbing at the wheel of my little blue Mini, as the stalled traffic hooted and steamed around me.

It was a warm day, the car's windows were open and, suddenly, a bunch of flowers was thrust through onto the passenger seat. A Cockney voice said, 'I don't know what you are crying for, darlin', but you're far too pretty to worry about anything.' Then he was gone. I had no idea who he was or what he looked like, but it was a heart-lifting gesture, and it turned out be an omen. Later that day I received a call telling me to prepare to fly to New York, where the show was already a great success, to be matched up with the leading man they wanted for the West End.

I subsequently discovered that the producers had decided on me to play Polly at my very first audition, and much of the delay was all about finding the right man to play opposite me. You never know what people are thinking, and can't really predict what your chances are. The thought processes of audition panels are rarely revealed to you and worrying about the logic or justice of their decisions is a waste of time. Auditions are just business, not personal. What we're trying to do here is alter the odds in your favour.

## Preparation for Your Audition

All you can ever really control is yourself: how well you've researched and rehearsed the role on offer, how well you listen to feedback, how easily you respond to direction, and ultimately how well you perform. Don't distract yourself with conjectures and theories about what a particular director or producer may want or prefer. Take a positive attitude, make your choices based on facts and, with meticulous preparation, you will know you've done everything you can. Getting ready for an audition can be divided into four basic actions:

1. The things you do consistently to build a healthy body and an active mind.

2. The practice you do every day to ensure your technique and performance is constantly improving. Aristotle said, 'We are what we repeatedly do. Excellence, then, is not an act, but a habit.'

3. The research you undertake about the specifics of each audition, so that the material you prepare is appropriate for you and the role you are going for.

4. The rehearsal of the material required for each audition.

*Body and mind*

We know it seems obvious, but as a musical-theatre performer, your body is your instrument. If you do not invest serious time ensuring it is cared for and well tuned, you will not succeed in your career. The demands on theatre performers increase with each passing year, and your stamina, flexibility and coordination are all crucial elements. Your mental health is just as important. How you feed your body and mind on a daily basis will have a huge impact on your success. Ask yourself the following questions (and be honest!):

• When was the last time you went to the gym?

• What was the last dance class you attended?

• How often do you practise your vocal exercises, or take a singing lesson?

• What was the last book you read that inspired you?

• Do you live on fast food, magazines and inactivity – or a regime of exercise, healthy foods and mental stimulation?

- Do you get enough sleep?

- Do you drink enough water?

Unfortunately, our business is not always conducive to a healthy lifestyle, which is precisely why you need to ensure you are always at your best. Prioritise physical and mental health and you can embrace auditions with a lot more confidence. You need to be at peak form to demonstrate your enthusiasm, good humour and ability in taking instruction and criticism.

Sometimes performers bypass chances with the excuse, 'I'm not ready.' This is because they only start real work *after* they hear of the audition. If you want to triumph, you must maintain a constant state of readiness. You never know when you may be called or when you might spot something you want to go for. Be prepared, like the Scouts. You should have audition pieces rehearsed to perfection that reflect your personality and show you off to best effect. Top athletes train methodically, not just for the race itself, and you've got to do the same.

### Daily practice

Aristotle's truism about excellence and habit is as true now as it was over two thousand years ago. A feature on a TV cookery show saw the best chefs in the UK competing with each other by trying to cook an omelette as quickly as possible. It was funny to watch because some of the experts got it spectacularly wrong. Why? Because they never cook omelettes. They are not exactly a regular feature on the menus of Michelin-starred restaurants. The ones who got it right had clearly spent time practising before their TV appearance.

There's no substitute, no secret and no trick that will replace practice. You must seek out instruction at the highest level right through your career, constantly developing technical and artistic knowledge. Skip one day and you'll notice; skip two days and your fellow students or colleagues will notice; skip three days and your next audition panel will notice! This can be hard, especially if you are also juggling a full-time job, but if musical theatre is to be your career, you will need to make time for the constant upkeep of your body and voice.

*Research*

Knowledge is power – and the more research you do in advance, the more likely you can walk into an audition with confidence and élan. The choreographer Stephen Mear's advice is: 'Do your homework. Find out everything you can about the show in question, the story, the creative team, the music – and be ready for anything. You never know whether somebody is going to ask you what you know about the show, even its history. It's not just about the acting, singing and dancing; it's about the whole production.'

Here is a checklist of questions you should ask before an audition if you can, either by speaking to your agent, the casting director or a member of the creative team:

- What role or roles are available in this particular casting?

- What is the story and style of the show I'm auditioning for?

- What is the musical range of the songs that the role/s I'm auditioning for must sing (soprano, alto, tenor, bass)?

- What has the audition panel specifically asked to hear (a rock song, a bluesy song, a Broadway belter or something operatic)? Do they want a monologue/speech?

- Will I need to dance as well as sing? Do I need dance or tap shoes or trainers?

- Is it a group audition or will I be seen on my own?
- Who will be on the audition panel, and what is their role in the production?
- Will there be an audition pianist?
- Are the panel asking for a particular look or dress style?
- If they've asked for specific material to be prepared, do they want it memorised?
- Will I be asked to sight-read or take part in any improvisation?

If you can, double check the details to make sure they are correct. Armed with the answers to these questions, you'll not only be able to perform with added confidence, but you're more likely to be relaxed and receptive to input and direction.

It's a lot to know, though. Many auditions happen at short notice and you'll be lucky to have more than a few days to prepare. The reality is that you can't cope in that length of time unless you are at the top of your game. In other words, you must have a collection of songs and monologues in a variety of styles perfectly polished, and you need to be fit and primed to take a movement or dance audition at short notice. If not, you are asking to fail.

## Choosing audition material

You can't possibly choose the right song or monologue to perform unless you've done enough research to know what style of piece will be appropriate. Your choice is crucial because it not only informs the panel about your under-standing of the role, but gives them clear messages about what you feel are your particular strengths. They can only assume you've chosen material that shows off what you do best, so it's important that you do precisely that. Choose stuff that fits you like a glove and highlights your strongest attributes as a performer.

It's a good idea to have *at least* half-a-dozen songs of differing styles ready to perform. If you have some idea of the show you're auditioning for, it obviously makes sense to sing something in a similar vein. But don't make the mistake of learning a new song because you think it might impress for that specific audition. You are far more likely to make your mark with a number your voice has really wrapped itself around than to attempt something completely fresh at short notice. There's a strong likelihood that you will not sing a new song as well as the ones you have been practising day in and day out. Equally, it is worth remembering that directors are listening not only for a voice that suits the role, but for a performer who cares enough to come well prepared.

It helps if your songs reflect your knowledge and understanding of the industry as a whole. By that, we mean that they are current and challenging, not out of date or completely inappropriate. You should avoid songs that have become overused or are singularly associated with one particular artist. The song that I sang as Fantine in *Les Misérables* (and with which Susan Boyle later became closely identified after stunning *Britain's Got Talent* audiences) – 'I Dreamed a Dream'– is a perfect example of a song that became overused for auditions and ultimately became a bit of a turn-off. Frank Sinatra's 'My Way' is so closely tied to the star that it is probably best avoided – unless of course it's been specifically asked for. Amazingly, I heard from one drama-school auditioner that some young people think singing 'Macavity' from Andrew Lloyd Webber's *Cats* is a clever choice. Maybe twenty-five years ago, but definitely not now!

Choose novelty or comic numbers with care. They sometimes won't show off your voice to your best abilities. Then again, some auditioners find them a refreshing change to the ballads they frequently hear all day long. Think about what is appropriate for the role and the musical.

Avoid material composed by yourself or a friend. No matter how good you may feel it is, it's ultimately subjective and unlikely to impress. Audition panels must make comparisons and choices between various artists and it makes their job simpler if you stick to good, mainstream work.

### Preparing audition material

When an audition panel asks for something specific to be prepared, make sure you receive it directly from them. You don't want to practise a song in the wrong key or with the wrong number of bars. Ask if they are expecting the song or scene to be memorised – but even if they say they are flexible, try to learn it anyway. Panels are inevitably more receptive to actors who have already made a serious investment in the job by knowing the words. It shows professional commitment. It will also encourage directors to ask more of you when there is not the distracting barrier of a script or sheet music between you and them. There are obviously going to be times when, at short notice, you need to read from the page but, if you have time to learn it, you should.

If you have been asked to sing a specific song, endeavour to work as much as possible with an accompanist prior to the audition. The more time you spend with a pianist, the less apprehensive you'll be on the day and the more flexible you'll be in responding to any change of direction that's asked of you.

### Interpretation

When practising any song, monologue or scene, it is of absolute importance that you know the exact context of the piece you're preparing within the framework of the musical.

How can you possibly deliver an intelligent or truthful version if you have no understanding of how it fits into the larger picture? At face value, any song or scene could be interpreted in an infinite number of ways unless you understand the significance of what precedes and follows it. Without that clarity, your preparation may be completely wasted. The more you know about how everything fits, the better your chance of offering up a good personal interpretation. If you can, read the entire play that a monologue comes from, or listen to the whole score of the musical from which you are singing a song.

Knowledge of past productions and performances can be valuable in studying for a role. Obviously, if it's a new musical, no previous performance exists and therefore you must use your own ideas in creating that character. But if you're auditioning for *Les Mis* or *The Phantom of the Opera*, both of which have been running in the West End for over twenty-five years, it would be reckless not to recognise certain performances and not know the whole show. Then again, if you're auditioning for the lead in *Cabaret*, you will want to be finding absolutely your own performance of Sally Bowles, not trying to recreate Liza Minnelli's. Replicating someone else's performance demonstrates a lack of imagination.

Audition panels want to hear what you can bring to the part that is unique and special. They'll take pleasure in discovering what your knowledge and imagination can bring to bear. Discovering new talent is always incredibly exciting and compelling, so don't muddle your best instincts by obsessing with the past performances of others in that role. Find your own voice – that's what will get you noticed and win you the job.

## Connection

When you're preparing songs, don't concentrate only on their musical aspect. Sometimes a melody is so strong or a rhythm so incessant that the intuitive expression of the words is lost to the power of the music. But the lyrics express the character's deepest thoughts and feelings, and it's essential that you connect emotionally with every word. If you want to create something truthful and move your listeners, then you must take care with the shape and energy of every single consonant and vowel. Find all the musical colours within the song and use the lyrics to tell the story.

When I auditioned to play Nancy in Sam Mendes' revival of *Oliver!*, he asked me to treat the song I was singing ('Maybe This Time' from *Cabaret*) as a speech, speaking the words without the rhythm, intonation and melody of the music. It's surprisingly hard to do, but a very liberating exercise to make sense of a song and create a deeper connection with it. When you come back to singing the song, you find that the words carry greater weight. The challenge and art of musical theatre is that both the music and the theatre must be given equal focus. Melody and lyrics stand side by side in value.

## Strengths and weaknesses

Remember that you are unique. There is no one else who looks or sounds precisely like you. Discover your strengths and play to them for all you're worth. You may be exactly what the auditioners are looking for.

Sometimes recognising your weaknesses can be just as important as knowing your strengths. Every performer has untapped talent which, given the right coaching and time, will flourish to become an eventual strength. But auditions are not the right time to demonstrate potential alone. They exist to evaluate what you can do best on the day, not what you hope to achieve in the future.

If the audition panel is looking for a tall, female, strong tap-dancer who can sing soprano in the ensemble, and you show up with only basic tap skills and a gravelly alto voice, you've just wasted your time and theirs. There's no point to going for things that you are clearly not right for. As one famous director friend of mine said, 'It's better to be remembered for something you can do than for what you can't do. You especially don't want to be remembered for wasting people's time!'

Imagine a panel that has one morning to audition fifty male dancers for a tenor ensemble in a new production. Not only do they need to shortlist the strongest dancers, they must also find the strongest tenor singers who can also act. Inevitably, there will be some who fall slightly short on the dance but are good actors with stellar voices, or vice versa. It is a tall order to determine who best fits the role in just a morning. It means that in the early stages, the panel might simply *ask* a candidate what their vocal range is or if they can execute a double pirouette rather than getting the individual to demonstrate it.

That's why it's so important to be clear what you can and can't do, what your dependable vocal range is, what your physical limitations really are, and that you answer truthfully any questions asked of you. If you are shortlisted for the next round of auditions based on exaggerated or false information, and then fail to hit that high C or turn a double pirouette on a dime, people are going to be very cross. They have no time to waste – and they may well remember you, for all the wrong reasons.

## CVs and headshots

As well as a prepared audition piece, you must also be able to provide, at short notice, an accurate CV and recent headshot. If you have an agent, they can do this on your behalf, but you should always have a supply of your own and keep them up to date. In this era of digital technology, there's no reason not to have both readily to hand. Your CV must comprehensively reflect your current experience, physicality and skills. Don't omit anything you have done or can do, but perhaps more importantly, don't include anything you haven't done. Exaggerations and white lies infuriate audition panels and most are very adept at sniffing them out.

Headshots are another sticking point with some panels, because sometimes the person standing in front of them at the audition bears little resemblance to the photo they are holding in their hands. The decision over who's invited to an audition is often based on headshots alone and yours must reflect what you look like now, and not what you looked liked three, five or ten years ago. Or, even worse, what you'd *like* to look like. I know one performer who had her photos touched up, literally out of recognition, and one casting director, comparing her with her photo, asked bluntly, 'Is this you?' 'Yes,' she squeaked. And he handed it back with a 'Thank you, that will be all.' So save the glossy glamour shots for your biography in the programme.

You should spend time and money getting your headshots right. Your picture may well be the first thing the producers see and will be the image they work from when putting their cast together. You don't have to pay the earth to get good-quality photos today, but you must get a professional to take them, and provide you with a contact sheet from which to choose your shots. You can find photographers listed in the directory *Contacts* (published by Spotlight), or ask your friends and colleagues for recommendations. There is more about getting the right headshots in Part Five.

## Before Your Audition

*Checklist*

Never store details about an audition in your head. It's a good ritual to write down every piece of information you must remember for the big day. It might seem elementary, but the memory can fail and you can't afford any hiccups. Your checklist should include answers to the following questions:

- What time is the audition?
- Where is the audition taking place, and what sort of venue is it?
- What is the casting agent's name and telephone number/s?
- What am I going to eat and drink before I go?
- What am I going to wear?
- How much time do I need for hair and make-up?
- How much time do I need to warm-up?
- How long do I need to travel to my destination?
- How am I going to travel to my destination?
- What will I do if I have travel delays?
- What do I need to take with me and in what bag?
- Do I have my up-to-date CVs and headshots ready?
- What music do I need?
- Is my music marked properly and clearly for the audition pianist?
- How will I quickly and efficiently instruct the audition pianist in tempo and cuts?
- Am I bringing dance shoes or extra clothing?
- If the audition lasts all day, what and where am I going to eat?

- What am I going to do to warm-up and stay loose right before I go in?

- How am I going to handle speaking to those registering me for the audition?

- How am I going to juggle running into fellow competitors, friends and adversaries?

Putting pen to paper can set a positive gloss on how you intend to handle matters. It not only ensures that you review and record everything you need for your audition, but you reduce the possibility of extra trauma and tension from forgetfulness when you need to be at your best. The simple act of setting out how you want this crucial day to evolve can establish a helpful mindset. What we imagine most vividly we can often go on to achieve.

*Sleep*

There aren't many difficult or stressful circumstances in life that aren't made better by a decent night's sleep. The amount and quality of sleep you have before your audition might just be another determining factor in how well you perform.

It is natural and expected to feel anxious, but alcohol, medication or drugs are not the answer to achieving a restful and rejuvenating night's sleep. It is quite common amongst those with artistic temperaments to try to burn or party away pent-up anxiety. It's important to find constructive ways of dealing with stress that will ultimately enable your body and mind to perform at optimum levels. You don't want to arrive for your audition looking as though you've been pulled through a hedge backwards. But some do. You'd be astonished how many will afterwards admit to partying the night before. This is either an act of reckless arrogance or thoughtless disrespect – and it always shows in the performance.

A good night's sleep will enable your body to use the adrenalin generated by the stress of the situation in a useful way. There's no magic number of hours one should sleep and the quality is just as important as the quantity, but you give yourself the best possible chance of performing at peak levels by ensuring that you are in a relaxed state of mind as you go to bed the night before your audition.

Make a point of getting to the audition room early because, apart from showing the right attitude, it might just get you a helpful earlier slot. There is nothing worse than feeling rushed or being late. Give yourself time to sleep, travel, warm up, and you've instantly improved your chances.

*Appearance*

What you wear to your audition is worthy of careful thought. Smart-casual clothing is generally acceptable; whereas flashy, over-the-top fashion statements and hairstyles should be avoided. There's no need to try and dress like the part you are going for, but what you wear speaks volumes about your care and understanding of the job on offer. A nice clean shirt, jacket and trousers will frequently look more appropriate than a scruffy T-shirt and jeans (unless you're auditioning for the chorus in *Hair* perhaps). If it's a period piece, girls might look better in a long skirt. Reasonable heels can add height and sometimes show off legs to an advantage, but make sure you can walk and move easily in them.

For men and women, whatever you wear, be sure you have complete freedom of movement. Leave any jewellery or piercings at home. Don't be too fussy. Keep it sensible, simple and be yourself. Don't try to be somebody you are not. Stephen Mear suggests that it is best not to dress just in black, but to wear something subtle, like a colour in your top or even a small neck scarf. It might distinguish you from the other auditionees and help the panel to remember you.

Make sure you dress in a way that does not upstage your own audition performance. Wear clothes that make you feel strong and confident, but remember, it's not the clothes the audition panel are ultimately looking at.

### Your Audition Day

*Audition bag and gear*

Preparing your audition bag should become a ritualistic habit best done the night before an audition. On the morning of the audition, you should be methodical and not hurry yourself. As we've said earlier, showing up without your music or the right gear might mean a wasted opportunity. If dance is involved, make sure you have all the stuff you need: jazz, point or tap shoes, leotards, leg warmers and so on. It's surprising how many people forget crucial items, and that lack of care and attention to detail gets noticed. So make sure you have everything you need before you set off for the audition:

- Directions to the audition venue
- Dance clothes
- Dance shoes and/or shoes to change into for the journey there and back
- Bottled water
- Food for energy
- Mobile phone – set to silent or turned off
- Wallet, money, keys, purse
- Script
- Sheet music

But travel as light as you can; don't turn up looking like you're going on holiday for a month.

*Respect*

Once you arrive, it's important that you behave respectfully to everyone, whether or not they are part of the administrative, managerial or artistic teams – or your fellow auditionees. These people may end up being your colleagues for weeks, months or even years! It's inevitable that in many instances, you will be kept waiting, sometimes for a very long time in less than comfortable surroundings, and you need to keep a check on any bad temper or annoyance that might creep in. These delays are rarely the fault of the staff organising the auditions and there's a fair chance that any rudeness will be reported up the line.

As a frequent audition panellist, Daniel has regularly heard of actors who have vented their frustrations and anger on the person signing them in at the door. It doesn't go down well. Directors and producers are looking for team players as well as talent for their productions. They like plenty of character, but not people who may become a disruptive influence or bring chaos behind the scenes. Showing respect to others is good manners and good sense. Take control of your temper or your temper could take control of your future.

## Your Audition

*Warming up*

Auditions are comparable to running a mile race and often last about as long. That's why it's essential that you always warm up thoroughly and drink plenty of water, both before and on the day itself. Our bodies prioritise by giving our vital organs water first, and the vocal cords are last on the list. So sipping water consistently throughout the day really does make a difference to the voice. Think of water as your melodically caring friend.

Try to find a corner where you can stretch and sing quietly so your body and voice remain loose and responsive. It's sometimes tempting to put off the impending moment by chatting too long with fellow performers, especially if there are friends there, but staying focused and in a state of readiness is absolutely essential. This is your business, your livelihood. Take it seriously and go in to win.

### In the room

When you enter the audition room, greet the panel brightly but don't be overfamiliar, even if you know some of them or have worked with them before. You're here to perform and compete. If they knew they definitely wanted you for the job, you would probably have been offered it without auditioning. You are on trial the moment you step into the room, so look as if you *want* to be there. The panel have a lot of people to get through, so always be prepared for a long, tense time. It's a frustrating, worrying, waiting game, but try to stay cheerful and hopeful throughout the day. This is the mood you should be radiating all the time.

When it comes to performing, stand tall and take a moment to breathe before you begin. Don't forget the power of stillness. When you're deciding where to direct your focus, think about the content and context of your pieces, rather than staring at a spot somewhere above the heads of the panel or directly into their eyes. Don't let their movement or reactions throw you off your stride. If you're offered different directions or instructions, follow them and seize the opportunity to try something new.

You may be asked some questions about what you've been up to recently, what you feel you have to offer the production, your thoughts on the character and so on. You could also be invited to put your own questions but don't worry if you have nothing to ask.

Auditions rarely run to time and the panel may spend quite a while with one person and very little with another. A long audition does not immediately mean particular interest; it can often indicate that the panel want to be sure they have seen the best of somebody. Just as surely, a short interview does not necessarily herald failure. If you've got what it takes, they will often know quite quickly, and may put you on a recall list straight away. In some instances, you're told immediately that you will or will not be recalled, and at other times, you will be notified solely through your agent. However you discover the result of the audition, it is never as cut-throat as television talent shows like *The X Factor*, with members of the panel pronouncing 'Yes' or 'No' in turn!

*Audition pianists*

Audition pianists are the closest thing you have to a friend in that room. Most top producers on big-budget productions spend a significant amount of their budget hiring pianists from a fairly small pool of players who know the repertoire, sight-read extremely well and are technically quite brilliant.

First and foremost, make sure you arrive at the audition with your sheet music in good condition and in the right key. Apart from the fact that it is careless and rude to expect the pianist to transpose from one key to another, you are opening up possible mistakes for both of you. Have your music properly marked and bound in such a way that the pianist can easily place the score on the rest and turn pages effortlessly. Make sure that there isn't a worrying wrestling match with paper.

Know precisely what instructions you want to give the pianist before walking into the room, and make sure you know how to point those instructions out clearly on the music. Not all pianists are perfect and you can't expect them to know exactly how to play the piece unless you take a few moments to set out what it is you want. Give them the tempo, any breaks and so on, but don't blame them if things go wrong – even if you do feel it is his or her fault. All eyes will be on how you interact with the pianist musically but also how you speak to them and take them through the music. If the tempo is not right at the start of your song, stop and ask politely for a slightly faster or slower pace. Don't be afraid, it would be foolish to get it wrong at this stage. When you're finished, regardless of what happens, thank the pianist, collect your music and bag, and leave the room brightly.

## Open auditions

Open auditions (sometimes justifiably referred to as 'cattle calls') can often attract hundreds or even thousands of performers. When I heard they were picking a cast for a revival of *A Chorus Line*, I was excited because I had just seen the movie with Michael Douglas playing the director – and had loved every second of it. On the day of the open audition, I was up at dawn and made certain I was number one of the 1,700 who auditioned that week. You rarely get to perform alone at open dance auditions and I made up my mind to be in the front and get noticed. Getting to the front is not being pushy. Somebody has to be there and there's no point in going to an audition if you don't want to be seen. Those at the back will be seen as well, but people instinctively like to see confidence.

For *A Chorus Line*, the first audition simply consisted of a time step and a double pirouette on each side. Auditionees were either out or put through based on that. In the second audition, we had to learn the routines, and if we got through that, *then* we had to sing. In all, I did five recalls for *A Chorus Line*. At the end, just as in the film, all the remaining performers were called onto the stage, and asked to step forward to be told if they had a job. I got the part of Maggie.

You'll find out about open auditions either from your agent, by keeping your ears close to the ground, checking on what productions are coming up and how they're being cast, or by looking in the industry press, like *The Stage*. Attend as many as you can. As always, get there early, dress appropriately, prepare thoroughly. Professionalism is the key; if you're late, hungover, difficult or nasty in any way, no one is going to employ you, even if you have the best belt in the business. Don't compare yourself to the other performers you see there; you are your own special talent. Concentrate like mad, learn the steps – and always look as though you're enjoying it.

## Your Attitude for Auditioning

*No excuses*

Audition panels *loathe* excuses. If you are not well or have another problem, either make the decision to carry on with the audition – or cancel. But don't bleat about it. Panels don't have the time or humour to hear about your mitigating circumstances. They are only interested in whether you are right for the job. Your recent illness, your lost music, the fact that you only heard about the audition yesterday or that you haven't had time to rehearse are lame reasons and they don't want to know. Just go for it or stay away.

*Fear*

Fear is a natural and inevitable part of performing. We all tend to imagine any number of possible embarrassing situations and sometimes magnify them into completely unrealistic worries. However, these fears can be managed and sometimes channelled to our advantage if we are properly prepared. The secret is to stay in control, not lose concentration for a second and not let your nerves get the better of you. It's tough, but it's what auditions are all about.

The people judging you know what you are going through and they want to see how you deal with it. And when you conquer fear there's a tremendous sense of exhilaration.

If the director asks you to do something, listen carefully and follow the instructions to the letter. If there's something you don't understand, query it. They want you to get it right and so should you. Don't be afraid to speak up.

If you do fluff a line, a song, a dance step, don't panic. Stop and ask if it is okay to start again, or restart at a point where you can continue with confidence. The audition panel wants to hear you at your best and will invariably be accommodating. Just make sure that second time through, you do it better.

*Courage*

Courage is the flip side of fear. As Oprah Winfrey once advised, 'Devote yourself today to doing something so daring even you can't believe you're doing it.' There is no better forum than an audition for venturing into uncharted territory. Directors love to work with brave actors, just as choreographers want to direct dancers who will dare. If you think it the right time, don't hesitate to draw the attention to any other edges of your talent you feel may prove useful to them. Be bold without being overly pushy.

My first major audition was for Lionel Blair, who was looking for dancers. During a break in running through the routines, I walked up to Lionel and asked if I could sing for him. He smiled at my chutzpah, and pointed out that there was no piano at hand. 'Never mind,' I told him, 'I'll sing without accompaniment.' Politely, he sat down to listen to me. I didn't get a job that day – but I left the room knowing I had done all I could.

While in New York, I auditioned for *42nd Street*. Beforehand, I borrowed a fur coat, learnt one of Dorothy Brock's scenes, and stepped straight into the speech for the audition panel. I did it right to the end and it was received with a long awkward pause before being asked to sing. I discovered afterwards that the Dorothy Brock part had already been cast and the deafening silence was because the panel were astonished and embarrassed I had tried so hard for a job that was not even on offer. But taking a chance – and looking foolish from time to time – actually does no harm. The theatre enjoys a splash of confidence, and it's impossible to survive working in it for very long if you care too much about your street cred.

## Positivity

Auditions are simply a means to an end, but it's a fact that most of those you attend you will not win. That is the reality of the business and completely unrelated to your worth as an artist. Casting a production is a human jigsaw puzzle and if you fulfil the requirements to be one of those pieces, you'll come out victorious.

The best thing you can do is stack the odds in your favour by not losing heart, and through relentless training and preparation. If you believe in yourself strongly enough, sooner or later you will make it. That's the excitement of the business. You never lose heart, you never give up, and one day your voice will be heard.

There's a pertinent lyric in Tim Rice and Andrew Lloyd Webber's *Joseph and the Amazing Technicolor Dreamcoat*: 'We all dream a lot; some are lucky, some are not. But if you think it, want it, dream it, then it's real. You are what you feel.' So *think* you'll win your next audition, *dream* you'll win – and maybe you will. With a bit of luck, the costume won't fit anyone else! Self-belief and a positive mental attitude are pre-eminent in achieving success.

## After Your Audition

Afterwards, go home and relax. Don't obsess and worry about every last event of the day. You've done your best, now see what happens next. You might be recalled and you might get the job and you can move on to preparing for the role – a euphoric moment.

But however good you are, you won't win every time and it can feel very personal when you don't. You face the agony of feeling rejected and wondering why you failed. Chances are that you haven't done anything wrong at all. The audition panel simply see somebody other than you in that particular part. There is no harm in asking the casting director or whoever if you went wrong in any way or if there is something you might do better in the future. You might pick up a crucial bit of advice. Whatever happens, accept it and move on.

It can be really hard to recover from the disappointment of losing an audition, especially the ones you come closest to winning. One of the roles that I really wanted – and felt absolutely right for – was Mary Poppins in the Disney/ Cameron Mackintosh stage version. I was one of the last couple of performers in the selection process when I heard that the producers were thinking of going with a younger actress. I was thirty-six at the time and remember the pain I felt when my agent called to say that they had 'gone another way'. It wasn't personal. I just didn't fit the image they had at the time.

If you don't get a part you really want, don't mope about it. Learn from the experience. Pick yourself up, dust yourself down, and get on with something else. I wasn't cast as Mary Poppins, so I did something better – I had another baby, my daughter Dolly.

The outcome of every audition is determined by the creative team and producers making subjective decisions based on what they feel is right for their show, and their decisions are based on what they feel is right for a particular role or roles. If you worked hard, did your best at your audition and come out empty-handed, you just have to shrug your shoulders and hope for better luck next time. It's the only way to go. If you've got what it takes, you *will* be found.

'Putting It Together'
Part Three: Rehearsing

# 3

# Rehearsing

## The Journey Begins

There are few feelings in the world as exhilarating as hearing you've got the job. Once you've been told the good news (and celebrated with your friends and family), you'll want to give the best performance possible, and bring something to the character that is memorable, regardless of whether you are taking over a role or creating it from scratch. Irrespective of whether it's a new or long-running musical, the rehearsal process is a tremendously exciting time. You'll now begin to work with a director, musical supervisor, musical director, choreographer, dance captains, stage managers and rehearsal pianists – not to mention your fellow cast members. It's a large and diverse group of artists, all uniting to turn the writers' words and music, presently on paper, into a living and breathing thing.

The other artists are your collaborators, but you will learn from them too. Each of them will provide important viewpoints, guidance and, in some instances, criticism. It is well worth listening to and analysing all of these so that you can fuse their experience and thoughts with your own to create a performance that is singular to you. The creative team of director, musical director and choreographer are the leaders of the rehearsal process, but it is your cooperation, understanding and inventiveness that will enable their inspiration to take flight. From this point forward, whether you're a principal player or ensemble member, your talent will become an essential ingredient in the extremely complex, rich and rewarding process. You have been employed to work as part of a team building up to a hopefully unforget-table opening night and a long, successful run.

In spite of the exhilaration of winning an audition and beginning to rehearse, make no mistake about it: the rehearsal process is something of an emotional roller-coaster ride, both personally and professionally. It can also be a double-edged sword. There's the excitement of being part of a new company, getting to know the cast and making a fresh group of friends, but creating your character can also be a difficult, stressful time. You are learning a lot of sometimes tricky material very quickly. Searching for what really works and what doesn't may prove a painful experience. It sometimes feels as though nothing is going the way it should and finding your feet is taking longer than you hoped. So, the more prepared you are going in to rehearsal, the easier some of the decisions will be to make. It's a tremendous help to know your lines and your songs, but even then, marrying the mind with the physical work takes its time and its toll. This is the purpose of rehearsals in the first place: to experiment, to try different options, to find the path you want to take with the character – and to keep practising until it's second nature. Be open to whatever suggestions are thrown your way; it's no bad thing to develop a reputation for being generous, open-minded and flexible in your attitude. But don't be afraid to speak up or offer ideas. They will mostly be welcome.

Being part of the creative process and working within an artistic family is ultimately why we're all in this business, and it's not uncommon to hear performers comment that the most enjoyable, meaningful part of being in any show is the rehearsal process itself. But to really relish that time, it is vital you bring your courage, invention and stamina into the rehearsal room and, perhaps most importantly, your preparedness!

## Rehearsal Preparation

Prior to rehearsals, you should receive both a piano/vocal score and a script (sometimes referred to as the 'book') from the production company, possibly via your agent. The score will contain all of the songs and scenes with the corresponding musical accompaniment, and the script will contain the dialogue and lyrics with no musical accompaniment. It is important that you work from both, regardless of whether or not you read music. Both the score and the script offer pathways into understanding the material, although, in some instances, you may appear to discover discrepancies between the two. You should identify and clarify any variations with the director. Are they mistakes or are there crucial lessons to be learnt about a character's motivation or emotions at these points? The divine is always in the detail and sometimes the deviation of a single word can have significant implications on a scene or a song. The sooner you've recognised any possible inconsistencies between the score and the script, the faster you'll be able to get on with creating the role and conquering your lines.

### Creating your role

You shouldn't aim to turn up on the first day of rehearsals with completely fixed ideas about how you are going to play your character. Rehearsals are the opportunity to work with the entire creative team and company on developing a performance that fits in perfectly with the whole production. But it's worth spending some time before rehearsals making a few early decisions about your character, and conducting research into your part and the world of the musical.

As you read through the script and score, and maybe listen to an existing cast recording, if there is one, then you can make some basic notes about your character as a useful checklist for when you enter rehearsals. Start by concentrating on factual questions – or the 'given circumstances' as the influential Russian director Konstantin Stanislasvky termed them – such as:

- What is your full name?
- How old are you?
- Where do you live?
- What is your relationship status?
- Do you have children?
- What do you do for work?
- How do you spend your spare time?
- What are your strengths and weaknesses?

After subsequent readings, and as you get more familiar with the character, the questions can get more probing, and might require you to use your imagination to fill in the gaps. Try asking yourself other questions that might be helpful, such as:

- What are your attitudes about race/religion/class?
- What are your strengths and weaknesses?
- What makes you happy?
- What makes you cry?
- Are you an optimist or pessimist?
- What are the best and worst things you have ever done?
- What quality would you change about yourself?
- What are your ambitions?

Other preparatory work you can do before rehearsals involves your attitude towards and relationships with other characters, which will considerably speed up developing the interaction on the rehearsal-room floor. Make a note of:

- Everything that your character says about themselves.

- Everything they say about other characters.

- Everything that other characters say about them.

It may help to keep these lists close to hand so you can immediately see how your character feels about another character when they meet in a scene.

The world of the musical can sometimes be very different from our own. If you are performing in a show set in a very different time or place, then it might be worth reading some books, watching films, looking at photographs or paintings online, or visiting exhibitions or galleries to get a better understanding about how those characters existed. You will be amazed how useful this can be. For example:

- If you're about to perform in *City of Angels*, it could be a help to watch movies from late 1940s Hollywood.

- If you're going to be appearing in *Fiddler on the Roof*, you might benefit from reading about early twentieth-century Russian pogroms.

- If you're performing in *West Side Story*, you could develop useful ideas about the environment, and your place in it, by looking at photographs of New York's Upper West Side in the 1950s.

This preparatory work and research can be a godsend, but don't fix your ideas, in case you find that they don't accord with the ideas of the director and the rest of the team once you get into rehearsal. Even if you don't do this sort of work beforehand, you should ask these questions of yourself and your character during the rehearsal process itself because they will probably help you create a much more rounded performance.

Unless specifically asked to do so, be wary of researching too closely any previous performances of the character you will be playing. Fastening on too tightly to earlier cast recordings or watching others acting on film – or even clips on YouTube – can inadvertently influence your own perform-ance. As soon as you start to copy what someone else has done, or is doing, you take away believability and, most likely, interesting new originality from the role.

*Learning your lines*

Before you put a foot in the rehearsal room on day one, you should familiarise yourself with as much of your material as possible. If you're in a brand-new musical, then there will almost certainly be rewrites to come, but that is no excuse for not learning the lines provided at the outset, even if you have to unlearn them later on. Likewise, if you're in the ensemble, you're unlikely to know yet what harmonies you will be allocated. But it helps to commit to memory as many of your lines and songs as possible, so that coming to grips with your character and understanding the story that the lyricist and composer are trying to tell will be that much simpler. It doesn't matter whether you have just ten notes of music or dozens of pages of songs and script, you need to know them pretty well because you have an obligation to the company. A company is just like an orchestra: if one instru-ment makes a mistake it can cause real discord, even in the early stages. You don't want to be that off-key instrument!

You have a responsibility to yourself and your own per-formance too. The director and musical director have much more to offer than helping you with your lines or finding the right notes to sing. That is the basic stuff you should com-plete prior to rehearsal, and it will be up to you to know exactly what's coming up and making sure you know your lines by then. There is nothing more frustrating than direct-ing somebody reading from a script.

Start by identifying all your lines and lyrics. Go through both the script and the score from beginning to end with a highlighter, mark every word and note of music that you must learn. This is not to say that you should arrive on the first day of rehearsals with a finished, fixed performance in mind. Quite the contrary; you need to be as open and receptive to direction as possible. But in order to achieve this, the sooner you are free of holding the script or music, the better. If there are existing recordings of the show you are preparing for, or videos on YouTube, then you may well find it useful to listen to or look at these to help learn the words and notes – it's a system I use myself. But, once again, be very careful not to let other actors' performances and vocal styles influence your own.

If you have any special skills or techniques to master (if you're lasso-throwing in *Oklahoma!* or roller-skating in *Starlight Express*, for instance), or have a new accent to acquire, then before rehearsals is also a good opportunity to practise those. Almost certainly you will get specialist tuition and time in rehearsals as well, but there's nothing like a head-start. Likewise, if you know you have to sing a sustained note at the top end of your range, or have to perform a complicated sequence of tap steps or high kicks, you should work on those disciplines too. You want to show people how good you are, and you can start to do this by being as ready as possible and thoroughly fit.

*Preparing your mind and body*

A typical rehearsal period might last four or five weeks; with a bigger show and a bigger budget it could be slightly longer. Over this time, every brain cell you possess will be tested to the limit and every muscle stretched to breaking point. You will also experience a wide range of emotions, from frustration and anger to jubilation. You will have to learn staging, choreography, dialogue and music, and you will create your own special character that gels with the vision of the director, the MD, the choreographer and the other actors. In addition to all of that, you'll have a new journey into work and once there you'll be dealing with unfamiliar people and coping with new personalities, new surroundings and new ideas. Stress-making life changes for some; exhilarating grist to the mill for others. But you've achieved your goal of getting the job, and the best route to making the dream come true is to stay physically as well as mentally ready for the very hard work ahead.

## Day One

The first day of rehearsals has arrived and with it come the mixed feelings of trepidation and elation. You are alone, but not for long because you will be meeting a group of other actors who have all survived the trials and tribulations of the auditions, vanquished their fears and triumphed by winning a job, just like you. It's a bit like the first day at a new school, but musical-theatre performers are invariably generous and affectionate people. By lunchtime, you will almost certainly be feeling quite at home. As a company, you are the new kids on the block and now the great adventure can really begin.

On day one of rehearsals, the room will be full of many more individuals than just your fellow actors, and a 'meet-and-greet' usually takes place where virtually everyone who has anything to do with the production is introduced: producers, director, music supervisor, choreographer, musical director, set, costume, lighting and sound designers, company management, stage management, wig and wardrobe supervisors, press and marketing representatives, sometimes the staff of the theatre, and possibly the writers themselves. It will be your first and probably last opportunity to meet absolutely everybody under one roof and on the same day, so make the most of it – and remember that first impressions count.

The first day of rehearsals of the Boublil/Schönberg musical *Miss Saigon* had a big impression on me. The cast was huge and the room was packed with people from all over the world. It had proved impossible to find enough Asian musical-theatre performers in the UK to play the Vietnamese characters, so producer Cameron Mackintosh had sent his team all over the world to find them. Seeing all these different cultures coming together in the one room was a unique experience – and very humbling, since many of the Asian actors were sending half their salaries back home each month to look after the families they had left behind. Whilst in London, many chose to live in cheap, cramped accommodation in order to save money to assist and support their families in their own countries.

After the meet-and-greet, you will usually be introduced to the designs for the set, costumes and wigs, and the director will often wrap up the introductions with a short speech outlining his or her aspirations for the cast and the production as a whole. Generally, at this stage, all personnel except for the directors and actors will go on their merry way to begin their own work on what can only be described as a 'mountain to climb'. Sometimes the team will stay assembled to hear the company's first readthrough of the whole show.

### The readthrough

Some directors like to begin rehearsals with a light-hearted game or improvisation to warm everyone up and get them in the mood for work. Others will dive straight into a readthrough of the script, sometimes accompanied by a sing-through of the songs by the musical director or perhaps the whole company.

The purpose of a readthrough is not for you to try and give a completely rounded performance, but for the whole company – and especially the director, musical director and choreographer – to hear, for the first time, the sound of the piece, to visualise the possibilities coming from this completely new combination of performers, and to gain at least some idea how this team will approach their roles and interact with each other. If the work is entirely new, the first readthrough also serves as an important milestone in the project because it may well be the first time the script has had life beyond the written word. In this instance, the writers will almost certainly be present, very probably scribbling notes about tweaks and rewrites they may want to make or consider later on. The initial readthrough tries to find the all-important connections, as well as the pace and rhythm of the piece, so any work you have done in advance is bound to be helpful.

First readthroughs, indeed the entire rehearsal process, can be considerably different between the West End and Broadway. In the UK, companies tend to spend time slowly opening up the piece and finding the characters, whilst in the US you might be up on the stage in a couple of weeks performing the whole thing, and then going back later to delve more deeply into the characters. Generalisations rarely stick in our business, and the exact opposite happened in the West End production of *Chicago*, where we were doing full runs of the show after just two weeks of rehearsals. In this particular instance, the Broadway production had already opened to great acclaim, so the creative team knew exactly what they were doing – and what worked – and got the London production up on its feet very quickly indeed. It was only then that we went back and worked through the show in much greater depth. Regardless on which side of the Atlantic you perform, there's no question that the rehearsal process is an uplifting, intoxicating and thoroughly nerve-racking time.

## The Rehearsal Schedule

Depending on the show, the director might begin rehearsals with improvisations to embed the world of the play in the company's subconscious or to explore emotionally charged or complex scenes. It's a wonderful opportunity to grow as an actor. Sometimes music or dance calls take precedence early on. Some directors work in chronological sequence; others pull a show apart into its individual sections and piece it back together only towards the end of the rehearsal period. Concurrent rehearsals are likely to take place throughout each day, so that scene work might be running simultaneously with dance rehearsals and individual music calls.

As a result, rehearsal schedules can often be quite complex and it's important that you carefully examine each day's timelines to determine when and where you're needed. If wardrobe and wig fittings have not already taken place prior to the start of rehearsals, they too will have to be squeezed into the schedule. This sometimes means you might miss important bits of rehearsal. If so, it's your responsibility to find out what you missed and catch up – in this respect it's a bit like still being at school or college.

The stage-management team is often juggling multiple rehearsal venues, so don't assume that the same rehearsals will always happen in the same studio. In fact, don't assume anything when it comes to scheduling and stay abreast of each day's diary. You don't want to be left floundering for an excuse about why you missed a rehearsal or wig fitting with stage management or, worst of all, with the director because you forgot to check the schedule.

Rehearsal studios will be marked out by stage management, with the stage space and the placing of set pieces delineated with tape on the floor, so that you can work within the actual parameters of the stage. Props and, in some instances, actual set pieces will be brought into the rehearsal studios so that, on the day you eventually move to the theatre, your surroundings feel pretty familiar and safe.

Although a company warm-up will often be conducted at the start of each new day, don't rely on it. You should be able and prepared to warm up by yourself, especially if you have long breaks in rehearsal when you are not being used. At the end of each day's rehearsals, examine the following day's schedule and make sure you are ready for what is coming up next. Trying to prepare whilst rehearsals are in progress is counterproductive to you and your colleagues. It's also sensible and useful to stay involved at all times, even when you're not being used – it's fascinating how much you can learn or develop just by watching other people at work.

## Your Attitude for Rehearsing

### Consistency

Directors want to see that the work you did in your auditions, the eye-catching stuff that led to your offer of employment, is well and truly in evidence in your daily rehearsal with them. Both Daniel and I have seen a number of instances where actors won an audition with a brilliant performance and then for some inexplicable reason it is never seen again – not in rehearsals, not in performance. This is a director's worst nightmare.

After getting the job, this is the time to bring into the rehearsal room any of the work you did with the creative team during auditions and use it as the starting point for discovering your performance. We understand perfectly that auditions are emotionally heightened experiences, but all your rehearsal work and eventual performance will demand this special commitment too. If it's not given, the director is going to be thinking that he or she made a very bad mistake – and might soon be scouring through their casting notes looking for your replacement.

## Self-belief

Once rehearsals start in earnest, the talent of the other performers will begin to reveal itself. Don't make the mistake
of comparing yourself with them. This is never a good thing
and can develop unhelpful feelings. A friend in New York
asked an Indian guru how she should achieve her goals. He
smiled and said, 'Think like a runner: keep your eye on the
finishing line and never look back. Stop comparing yourself
to others. If you glance behind to see how the others are
doing, you may fall and fail.' It's good advice. By all means,
study the things you admire in other actors or singers, but
always remember that you have been chosen for your own
particular qualities.

Equally important in rehearsals is learning to let go of any
inhibitions. Allow yourself to experiment, take risks, try new
things. This time is so precious it's a crime to waste any of it
on being guarded or trying to remain invulnerable.
Unshackle yourself, let loose your imagination. The entire
creative team is there to support you in that aim. They too
want to be inspired, so don't be afraid. Between you and
them, you may well find something very special.

## Stamina

Rehearsals can be a stressful time for both your voice and
your body, so it's important to know when to give your all
and when to conserve energy. Always endeavour to find a
system and balance that continually pushes you towards
greater stamina. A number of times Daniel has seen well-
known people, who have never performed onstage, cast in
leading theatre roles. Mollycoddled and sheltered throughout rehearsals by their own teams and managers, some have
subsequently been unable to perform on opening night
because they've lost their voice or, later, prove utterly incapable of delivering eight shows a week because they don't

have the essential strength to survive a normal performance schedule. And, believe me, you need it.

Experience has shown it's not just some celebrities who can be found wanting in this fundamental way. This is why we lay so much importance on establishing a really robust work ethic that will give you the sinew you will undoubtedly require to survive opening night and beyond. The voice is made up of the muscles of the larynx, air, space and the articulators (tongue, teeth, palate, lips). Just like any group of muscles, the more you exercise them properly, the more they strengthen and progress. As with everything else, though, you have to look after those vital cords and, hopefully with advice from your voice coach, develop a technique of singing founded on relaxation and release. Short of a complete rest, a shift to good breathing and relaxation will go a long way towards improving inflamed vocal cords.

Exercising your voice is something you must continue with for as long as you intend to make a living that way. This is advice I understand only too well, having foolishly ignored it in the past. Not long ago, I was doing a number of non-singing roles for some time – a straight play, some TV, some voice-overs – and then, suddenly, I was required to do an important charity concert at short notice. I had several rehearsals in the days beforehand, but my voice had relaxed from lack of use and, after singing eighteen numbers in about two hours, I had lost my voice next day. Now I trill a bit each day without fail.

It's also necessary to use your common sense during rehearsals; make sure you don't waste your energy and voice unnecessarily. If there's a lull, that's not the time to demonstrate back flips or give your new Liza Minnelli impression, only to find you are at less than your best in the subsequent scene. When Daniel was working on *Mary Poppins* in Las Vegas he was a guest at one of the famous gambling town's many casinos one night, and was shocked and alarmed to see a dancer from the show practically bouncing off the ceiling. Next day the performer was virtually incapable of lifting a toe in rehearsals. This lack of intelligence and professionalism is a real turn-off for producers and directors who pour effort, not to say money, into trying to create something very special.

## Professionalism

Don't be late. Rehearsals must be a bit like being in battle, with some terrifying and exhilarating moments followed by long periods of waiting. Don't be late for the battle and don't be caught asleep when the action starts. Good timekeeping shows respect and gets noticed. If you're five or ten minutes early, you're on time. Once in rehearsal, stay alert and warm so that when called upon, you are immediately at your best. Always keep stage management informed as to your whereabouts and be respectful of ongoing work you're not involved in. Keep your chat down to a whisper or stay completely silent, depending on the sensitivity of the space and circumstances.

Make sure your mobile phone is turned off or silent whenever you step into the rehearsal room. There are directors who impose a penalty fine of £5 (or more) on those who let their phone ring. The money collected during rehearsals is usually put towards drinks or treats at the first-night party.

## Working with the Director

The best directors always strive to create an atmosphere and environment that allows the company to be free and experimental in creating their performances. But on opening night, it's the director's concept of the entire production that will ultimately triumph or fail, so it's essential both artistically and professionally that you listen to and trust their judgement.

The director is the ultimate boss; he or she has a vision of how they see the show and how you fit into it. Of course, they will want you to find your own facets and qualities in the role, but never try to take things into your own hands – as I did when I was creating my performance as Roxie Hart in *Chicago*. After weeks of being directed, I began to feel Roxie was becoming too much of a caricature. I wanted to strip it back to the sleek lines of Bob Fosse and stop worrying about putting too much extra on top of that. I discussed these reservations with the director, Walter Bobbie, but perhaps didn't explain myself as well as I might have done; very sensibly he wanted it played as he had directed it on Broadway. Somewhat impetuously, I took matters into my own hands and performed the role my own way at the first preview. It sent the whole creative team into meltdown and I received the dressing-down of my life. I went back to playing it the way they wanted and the show was a great success; I got the chance to reassess the role and get deeper under Roxie's skin when I played her in New York and at a special tenth-anniversary performance in London. So don't be afraid to speak up if you feel something does not work or if you can add something beyond what you've been asked to do, but always channel it through the director, so that their vision is always taken into respectful consideration.

It's quite possible that you may be directed to do something that initially feels uncomfortable. Sometimes it's what you're asked to wear that you'll find most difficult. Some of the 'Vietnamese' girls in *Miss Saigon* were initially not happy with the idea of appearing onstage in bikinis, but had their worries eased away with a clear explanation from director Nicholas Hytner of why it was essential to the storytelling. Never be afraid to ask a director for more clarification if you genuinely feel that what is being asked of you is inappropriate. Ultimately, you must be the custodian of your own ethical boundaries: don't ever allow a director – or anyone else for that matter – to bully you into doing something you believe is wrong.

## Rehearsing Your Performance

The very fact that you've been hired to play a particular role in a show means that the creative team has seen something in you, both as an actor and a person, that fits their idea of who that character should be. If the director is looking for a killer or someone contemplating murder (say, Jud Fry in *Oklahoma!*) he or she is not, of course, looking for someone who is, or even looks like, a homicidal maniac. The choice will be an actor seen as capable of peering into the darker realms of their own psyche in search of somebody with the capacity to kill.

Roxie Hart, the girl who pumps her lover full of lead in a moment of passion, is a role to kill for. She'd do anything to become a star and that was a big part of my route into finding her personality: my own determination to becoming successful myself. Our shared ambition served as my doorway into a deeper understanding of Roxie's aspiring, one-track mind. As you do the pre-rehearsal work described earlier, see if you can find the common links between you and the character. They could turn out to be important touchstones as you develop your performance.

Plenty of techniques have been developed over the years to assist actors in creating roles. Some of these will be prescribed by a director in rehearsals. He or she might be an advocate of the actioning process, for instance, or like to do lots of off-text improvisations. At other times, the director will not employ any specific technique to help you build your character, except for a more generalised process of repetition, note-giving, discussion of the role, and then trying it again. All of these are valid ways of approaching the task and ultimately you will have to be led by the process that the director favours. But there are certain things you can try out for yourself to see if they help you create a character. You might be able to do some of them working alone in your own time or, possibly, get together with other actors after rehearsals. There are books galore detailing these different styles and processes. Here is a brief outline of some ideas you might encounter or want to explore.

## Units and objectives

The Russian theatre director Konstantin Stanislavsky was the first to develop a complete system for acting. In part, it is aimed at helping actors access and use their own memories to get right into the emotions of a character. In this sense, the actor does not so much become someone else as much as he or she finds where their character – and their character's emotions – are already within him or herself. The system has been described in many different books, not least Stanislavsky's own, and it is certainly worth reading his two seminal texts, *An Actor Prepares* and *Building a Character*.

One of the most fundamental techniques of Stanislavsky's system was the principle of breaking the text down into individual units. You can do this for both scenes and songs, dividing the words and lyrics into short chunks, with each unit containing a single objective – or 'want' – for that character. This want might be very specific and rooted in the text: for example, Oliver wants some more gruel and to find a family and security; the nuns want to solve a problem like Maria; Galinda wants to make Elphaba popular.

The super-objective is the overarching desire or want that propels the character through the whole show: Dorothy wants to find a way back home to Kansas, the Scarecrow wants a brain, the Tin Man wants a heart, the Lion wants courage, and so on. In musicals, the principal character's super-objective is often revealed in an 'I Wish' song towards the start of the show: for example, the Little Mermaid's 'Part of Your World'; 'Where is Love?' from *Oliver!*; 'I Hope I Get It' from *A Chorus Line*.

Once you've identified what your character wants, you need to pinpoint what stands in the way of achieving it (the obstacles) and then how to set about getting it (their actions). Identifying your character's overall super-objective, the moment-by-moment targets, and his or her action plan may well bring added depth and believability to your performance. You need to develop the motivation that makes you say that line or move onstage at that particular time.

### Magic if

The 'Magic If' is another idea of Stanislavsky's, to help actors put themselves in their character's situation. At its heart it involves asking yourself 'What would I do *if* I were in the same situation?' By asking – and answering – this question you can often connect with your character and develop a more thoughtful performance. Here are some more specific examples: 'What would I do *if* I had fallen in love with a girl from a rival community?' (Tony from *West Side Story*); 'What would I do *if* I fell in love with my boss?' (Maria in *The Sound of Music*); 'What would I do *if* my plant had eaten my girlfriend?' (Seymour in *Little Shop of Horrors*).

### Subtext

Sometimes, mainly in solo songs, characters will reveal their deepest, most private feelings; for example, Tony's 'Maria' from *West Side Story*; Billy Bigelow's 'Soliloquy' from *Carousel*; or Audrey's 'Somewhere That's Green' from *Little Shop of Horrors*. But, more often than not, we don't always say exactly what we mean. Beneath our words are hidden thoughts that we don't show because they are too painful, revealing, private, embarrassing or inappropriate. This is our subtext and it features in drama as much as in life. You can work through your script thinking about and considering what is actually motivating the words that your character says and driving their actions. The important thing to remember is that you shouldn't overtly *play* the subtext in performance. Detailed, sophisticated acting is about keeping it 'sub'. But if you're thinking it, the audience should sense it and feel it.

### Hot-seating

A popular rehearsal technique, practised by directors of both plays and musicals, is hot-seating. One actor is in character and the rest of the assembled company asks them questions about their life, their objectives, their motivations, their subtext. These questions can be quite generalised ('What do you do for work?'... 'Where have you come from today?'... 'Tell us about your family'...) to the very specific ('Why do you paint your fingernails green?' to Sally Bowles from *Cabaret*; 'Why do you dislike children so much?' to Miss Hannigan from *Annie* or Miss Trunchbull in *Matilda*). You might not have actually thought about the answers to some of these questions when you're asked them, which means you will have to improvise in the moment. As a result, the exercise ensures that you are developing a solid, three-dimensional character.

### Actioning

The process of actioning, which also develops from Stanislavsky's system, is where you apply a verb (a 'doing word') to every line of text, or to each unit. The verb should be transitive – so that it is an action that you do to the other person with whom you're interacting; e.g. 'I *enchant* you', 'I *accuse* you', 'I *corrupt* you', 'I *energise* you', and so on. The point is that it helps you to find something very specific and playable towards the other character on each line; rather than something that's repetitive or superficial. Changing the action should change the nuances of how you're playing a certain line, and make the performance specific and spontaneous. You can always vary the action throughout rehearsals and once you've begun performing the show.

Take the great song 'Anything You Can Do' from Irving Berlin's *Annie Get Your Gun*, in which two rivals playfully square up to one another, attempting to outdo each other in a series of tasks. The same refrain 'Anything you can do I can do better; I can do anything better than you... No, you can't... Yes, I can... No, you can't...', etc. is repeated throughout the song. Without finding a different impetus behind each line it will become generalised and boring. So try playing each 'No, you can't...' and 'Yes, I can...' with a different action; e.g. 'I *defy* you', 'I *challenge* you', 'I *reject* you', 'I *confront* you', 'I *beguile* you', 'I *humour* you', 'I *charm* you', and so on. Although some of these actions might be virtually synonymous, there is a slightly different flavour or colour to each word which will bring something new to how you play it. The technique is used by many actors rehearsing dialogue in plays, but is also a useful system for preparing a song where lyrics are repeated and when you don't want to play it the same each time.

## Animal work

Actors can make useful discoveries about character by observing animals. When I was in *Children of Eden*, the team made regular excursions to London Zoo to observe the many different creatures we were playing in the musical. I took an interest in cats when reading about them while appearing in the Lloyd Webber musical of that name. They are fascinating, independent creatures, and I eventually became the proud owner of Jeremy (an English cream) and Jemima (an English blue), who was a beautiful blue-grey colour. Later, when I was in *Miss Saigon*, I had to take them to the theatre because it was Christmas Eve and I was travelling on to my parents' home in Suffolk straight after the show.

Some of the girls in the ensemble adored them and let them out to run loose in the dressing room, unaware that the Theatre Royal Drury Lane has undergone all sorts of internal alterations in its long history. Needless to say, during the interval, my two precious cats found a hole in the wainscoting and disappeared. They defied all entreaties and encouragement, and were still lost somewhere in the bowels of the playhouse when the show came down. Several hours later, they were still missing. Leading lady Claire Moore and her dresser stayed with me as I sobbed, mewed and called into the echoing, empty theatre. The theatre fireman eventually nipped out to a restaurant and returned with a large sardine. This we dangled down the hole, and a little while later, Jeremy and Jemima reappeared – no longer cream and blue, but absolutely filthy black. I now have a dog, Poppy, a little white Schnauzer, who keeps me fit on long walks. I will see to it that she is left firmly at home any time I am called to Drury Lane.

### Improvisation

Some directors will use improvisation in rehearsals to explore events that happen offstage before the start of the musical or in the gaps between scenes. They are a useful opportunity to free up your creativity and to develop the part you are playing using your own words, thoughts and actions. Almost always, improvisations will lead to a deeper understanding of your character and his or her situation in the whole show.

For example, the premise of *Mamma Mia!*, the popular ABBA jukebox musical, might easily provide interesting material for a series of improvisations. The show is about a woman living on a Greek island being reunited with several of her former partners. It would be fun to explore the moment that Donna first meets each of these partners, Sam, Bill and Harry. The actors will then have a stronger, more specific sense of the story behind each relationship: how they met, why they were attracted to each other, what were the best aspects of their relationship and so on. Likewise, it would be productive to act out when and how each of those relationships ended so that, when they first meet onstage, the actors can recall that moment their characters last saw one another.

The first rule for improvisation is not to be self-conscious and not to worry about delivering a performance or entertaining any onlookers. If you are concerned about making a fool of yourself and you don't take risks, then you won't achieve anything. Secondly, you should never 'block', which means that if another actor comes up with an idea in an improvisation then you should just go with it. Don't shy away from it or deny it. If it forces you to do something 'out of character' then you can always discuss it afterwards and then try again. But frequently in improvisations, as in life, the richest rewards come when you're daring.

*Rehearsing your music*

At first, you will probably rehearse your songs separately, in a different room from the main rehearsals, and with the musical director and a rehearsal pianist present. Learning the musical score often takes precedence in the first week or two of rehearsals. It can be useful to carry a Dictaphone or digital sound recorder (actually, most mobile phones today can perform the function) to record your vocal line or the piano accompaniment, so that you can practise at home.

Once musical notes and scenes are learned, the priorities begin to shift to character, in addition to rehearsing scenes of spoken dialogue which usually are the sole domain of the director. However, often the director and musical director will work in tandem, exploring and honing your dramatic and musical performance together. Then, working with the choreographer will add a further exciting element to the jig-saw puzzle of your musical and dramatic performance.

Every composer, every musical and every song demands dif-ferent things of its performers. In general, the same techniques for preparing spoken scenes (actioning, finding the subtext, and so on) can also be applied to rehearsing your songs. The exercise of performing your song lyrics aloud as spoken text, without the melody or rhythm of the music, really helps connect you with the words you are delivering.

You will also have the added considerations of controlling your breathing, planning your phrasing and dynamics, and developing the colour, tone and timbre of your voice. The director and musical director will have strong ideas on these elements, and will work on them with you during rehearsals. As rehearsals progress, your songs will gradually be inte-grated with the scenes and choreography, so that all the elements are brought together into a cohesive whole.

## A word of warning

All these different rehearsal techniques are aimed at getting deep underneath a character's skin and developing a per-formance that the audience will find right on the mark and affecting. But you must be extremely careful not to blur the boundaries between yourself and your character too realis-tically, especially if you're tackling an all-consuming role, as I did when playing Marguerite.

My older sister Noel had died just a few weeks before we went into rehearsal for *Marguerite*, and unsurprisingly, I was emotionally hurting. My character goes from a charmed life as a high-class courtesan to being raped, beaten and finally killed as a Nazi collaborator in occupied France. I wanted the effects of being physically assaulted to be as real as pos-sible, and told the actors playing my assailants not to treat me like a china doll. Underpinning my instructions to the attackers was the thought that a bit of rough handling might not only help me forget my sadness, but could even heighten my performance. For eight shows a week, I was thumped, shaken and thrown around the stage, eventually suffering bad tendonitis in both my elbows and ankles, and a bursa in my shoulder, not to mention an assortment of bumps and bruises. Furthermore, crying a lot over the death of my sister and faced with incredibly demanding songs and scenes, I ended up straining my larynx.

Physically and vocally in trouble, I realised that using my sorrow to 'enhance' my portrayal of Marguerite was only scratching the wound, night after night, of losing my sister. It was not enabling me to perform the character better, indeed it was doing damage to me on every level. We must never forget that truth onstage is quite different from truth in real life. Actors must not actually believe in the veracity of events onstage, only in the imaginative creation of them. Somewhere along the way, I crossed that line. It was quite literally a painful lesson to learn, but an important one. You need to acquire the techniques of acting and maintain a clear gap between real and stage life.

## Different Types of Role

### Principals

If you're playing a principal or leading role, you'll have just one part to learn and make your own – but it might carry the weight of the whole show and involve lots of scenes and musical numbers. You'll have plenty to do perfecting these and, in creating that special character, you will also find that every second of your rehearsal time and beyond will be spent thinking how you are going to do this. It will completely consume your life – and rightly so. A lot of money and quite a few careers may be riding on the success of your performance.

You may have a leading role in the show and bear a large chunk of the responsibility, but that does not make you superior to the rest of the company. Behaving like a diva will win you no friends – and will certainly not help your career.

As a principal player, you are likely to have at least one and possibly two understudies to cover you in case of illness, injury or holiday. I understudied Claire Moore in *Miss Saigon*, who was especially thoughtful to me, always giving me good warning if she was going to be off, so that I could invite friends, family or my agent, and leaving flowers and champagne as a gift the first time I covered her role. It proved a lasting lesson about how to treat understudies.

*Ensemble*

If you've been cast in the ensemble, you will probably be understudying one or more principal roles, but your ensemble role remains vital to the success of the whole production. As thrilling as it is to step up into the part you understudy, all of your moves and lines in your ensemble role are essential parts of a complete picture. We should constantly bear in mind the old saying: 'There are no small parts; only small actors.'

Of course, your primary responsibility as an ensemble player is to learn and perfect your role or 'track', the term given to all the actions, choreography and vocal lines that you perform throughout the show. Your track may see you playing a range of different characters in different locations, and often these will be unnamed. It is generally helpful to create personas for these individuals – which will not only give you something richer and more specific to play, but also be more fun to perform each night. It's very hard, for example, to play an 'unnamed, anonymous, generic factory worker' in *Les Misérables*, and far more interesting if you create a whole character, working out what it is exactly that you do in the factory, where you go home to at night, who your family are, what your attitude is to those in power in France, and so on – even though the audience will never find out all of these exact details. If you don't do something along these lines, your performance will become superficial and stereotyped – and the audience *will* notice that. You'd be amazed – there's always somebody with their eyes on you.

## Understudies

If you are understudying a principal role, this obviously means learning two parts: your ensemble role and the leading one. Don't make the mistake of waiting for individual understudy rehearsals to begin before learning both your roles. It's vital that you prepare before and after rehearsals, so that during them you can focus entirely on direction rather than line-learning. Always confirm with stage management and the director that you are permitted to sit in on principals' rehearsals, and do so when and wherever possible. This way, you can begin to gather the information you need to play that particular role from the director him or herself, rather than one of their assistants at a later date.

The strength and solidity of your work during rehearsals will be noticed by all, and you never know when opportunity will come knocking on your door. Claire Moore understudied Sarah Brightman as Christine in the original cast of *The Phantom of the Opera*. During previews, Sarah lost her voice but Claire, word and song perfect, was able to step straight in, preventing the cancellation of the performance. These emergencies happen more often than you might think and stars have been born on just such occasions – but only if they have done their homework.

Sometimes you'll have many roles to learn. I understudied four different parts in *Cats*, including Grizabella with her wonderful hit song, 'Memory'. *Cats* was a particularly tough show on dancers, so cast members were often off with injuries. In the twenty months I was in the show, I barely played Jemima, the role I was cast in, because I was so frequently on for someone else. Understudying is never boring, allowing you to stretch your wings into different, probably bigger roles, and teaching you how to become so much better at what you do.

As an ensemble member of a cast, always be respectful and supportive of all the principal performers; ultimately, it will be in your own best interest. When the time comes for you to step into the role you are understudying, you'll want and need to be treated as an equal. Put another way, 'Do unto others as you would have them do unto you.' Show support and respect – and you'll get it back.

Whether you're an understudy or playing a principal role, if you get all the material absorbed into your system it will stay with you, not necessarily for ever, but certainly for a long time. Some time after I had left *Les Misérables* and done other work, I got an urgent call from Cameron Mackintosh's office: could I possibly take the stage that night in my old role of Fantine? The girl playing the part was away on holiday, the first understudy was sick, the second understudy dealing with a family bereavement, and the third understudy was also unwell. Fortunately, they caught me in a brief spell between jobs and I went straight to the theatre, had a quick rehearsal, and was onstage that evening and again the following night. It was a lovely feeling and, in a strange way, just as if I'd never been away – even though a number of the cast were quite different.

It was done so quickly that there wasn't even time to slip a note into the programme to say I would be playing Fantine. Friends of my family who happened to be in the audience that night – and presumably missed the announcement about the change – were amazed when I turned up onstage. During the interval, they asked what was going on and were told by theatre staff.

Remarkably, something similar occurred after I had left *Miss Saigon*. When I was on a break in New York, the show was ending its long run there but, because business boomed on the announcement of the closure, the decision was taken to run the show for an extra month. However, the actress playing Ellen was moving on to a new contract elsewhere and they needed somebody at short notice to step in. It was the role I had played in London, I was on hand and so I performed in the great musical through to its last night on Broadway.

## Swings

A swing's job is to step in whenever another member of the ensemble cast is off work, either on holiday or sick, which means that female swings must know every female track and male swings must know every male track. Occasionally a swing will be asked to understudy a principal role, but rarely at the start of their employment, because there will be so much material for them to learn that it's extremely easy to feel overwhelmed, especially if they've never done it before.

The most important thing is not to panic. Always seek out the advice of the dance captain, the member of the company responsible for maintaining the artistic standards of all the production's choreography, and get organised. Be methodical in how you tackle learning each track and take detailed notes. Don't try to learn everything at once. Most people's brains just don't work like that. Take it one step at a time and grab every opportunity you can to get up and mirror the track you're learning. Swings are vital for the smooth running of a show and have the tremendous responsibility of slipping into any role at the last minute and getting it absolutely right. It's awe-inspiring what they achieve.

## Different Types of Production

The rehearsal process will vary quite significantly depending on whether you are part of an entirely new company working towards the opening night of a fresh production, or taking over a role as part of a cast change in an ongoing production. A third scenario is that occasionally, due to personal or professional circumstances, a single ensemble track or principal role might become available, and you'll be the only new cast member to break in. Each circumstance is different and will have varying rehearsal schedules.

### New productions

Rehearsing as one of the original cast of a new production is thrilling. There's an incredible feeling of becoming part of the blueprint of that show – and there are very few things that compare to being the first person to create a character. In cooperation with the writers, director, MD and choreographer, you will be rehearsing scenes, musical numbers and dance routines that are still in the process of evolving and being refined. For this reason, rehearsal times for new shows are usually longer. *Children of Eden* rehearsed for the best part of three months; *Miss Saigon* for about two.

Over this time, it is common for entire numbers or routines to be cut, rewritten or rethought. Each day of rehearsals might bring new lyrics to work on, text to rehearse, or choreography to learn, so you will require maximum flexibility and a great deal of patience. Unquestionably, new shows foster greater overall creativity for cast and crew alike, but the constantly evolving creation can have its victims. In *Miss Saigon*, the big song for Ellen (the part I was understudying and later took over) changed musically twice and lyrically four times. Overall, the role was continually being cut throughout the rehearsal period because the show was too long. These sorts of changes are an inevitable reality when rehearsing an entirely new musical.

I found being in the world premiere production of *Marguerite* a particularly rewarding experience because I was involved from a very early stage. Based on the novel *La Dame aux Camélias* by Alexandre Dumas *fils*, with book and lyrics by Alain Boublil and Claude-Michel Schönberg, and music by Michel Legrand, I was brought in practically at the start to sing through the songs for the show. This led to involvement in the workshop, and ultimately in the first full production at the Theatre Royal Haymarket in 2008. But first there were months and months of writing and rewriting; one song had three completely different sets of lyrics before the team felt they had got them just right. With co-stars Julian Ovenden and Alexander Hanson, I would sit with Jonathan Kent, the director, adjusting the script and sorting out what we thought needed to be said at certain points within the script. It meant that we felt great ownership over our characters, which were tailored to our voices and personalities.

The allure of being part of a new show is absolutely beguiling, but make no mistake that the brutal reality of our business is that quite a lot of new shows fail. The rewards of taking part in a new production are potentially great, but the risk will always be there that you might be looking for a new job very soon after opening night.

## Takeovers

At any given time, London and New York will usually have a similar number of shows that have been running for longer than a year (sometimes the very same shows are running on both sides of the Atlantic). The US, and to a lesser extent the UK, also have multiple touring productions of musicals too. As the personal and professional circumstances of those casts change, some actors inevitably move on, job opportunities are created, casting calls are held, and new members will be hired and rehearsed into the production. Generally, these rehearsals will be conducted by the resident director, who is employed to attend performances and keep a watch over the show in the absence of the director, who by now has probably moved on to another show or shows. However, if it's a full cast change or you are playing a principal role, you would hope to have some contact with the original director.

In London, a one-year contract is standard, meaning that a cast change will occur every twelve months with a rehearsal period to integrate new cast members into the production alongside those who have decided to extend their contracts. In New York, cast members are hired for the run of the show and unless they decide to move on to another production, they have the right to remain in the role for as long as it runs on Broadway. This scenario is far more advantageous to the original cast: it provides some semblance of personal and economic stability whilst the show runs, but can bring with it some lethargy as time goes by. It also reinforces a situation where new talent is left struggling to find a way into that specific production and the business as a whole. Finally, not everyone who leaves a show leaves voluntarily, and sometimes you might be replacing someone who has been asked to leave.

Regardless of which continent you live on, taking over a principal, ensemble or swing role in a long-running musical means rehearsing in a slightly more specific way. There will be no last-minute changes of lyrics and no new scenes or routines to learn at the eleventh hour. Your role – or track – is now fixed in the production, but that does not mean that you cannot bring something original to the show. Indeed, any good resident director looking after a long-running show will positively encourage you to be as individualistic and imaginative as possible. They will know that new input and ideas will inspire remaining cast members and help to reinvigorate the entire production. Indeed, when taking over a role, it's important to make your mark and bring something to the table that doesn't simply slip into a pre-existing performance. Thankfully, no role is ever set in stone. Different directors and actors will always find new things to explore in any given part. The role of Hamlet has been performed thousands of times, for instance, but no one in that role plays it in the same way; not Henry Irving, Laurence Olivier, John Gielgud, Mark Rylance, Mel Gibson, David Warner, Ethan Hawke, Jude Law, David Tennant – not even David Tennant's understudy, Edward Bennett, who went on when David was injured – would have played it the same way. The same is true of any musical-theatre performance.

When a large number of the cast are taking over from current performers, your final two weeks of rehearsal will fall very similarly into line with the final weeks of a brand-new production – in that you will rehearse scenes with remaining cast members and then move into the theatre for technical and dress rehearsals as usual. What will differ is that the rehearsal process will be more condensed and you will be integrating with colleagues who already know the exigencies and intimacies of the production. If you are one of the cast remaining with a show, you should use the influx of new cast members to really re-examine your own character, and find new avenues to develop and evolve your own performance.

Taking over a role as the *only* new cast member in a long-running production is daunting but quickly rewarding. Chances are that the producers will want you in the production as soon as possible, but unfortunately, being the only one rehearsing doesn't mean that choreography, songs or dialogue go into your brain or body any easier. Yes, you will have all the individual attention of the resident team in rehearsals, but you will also have the pressure to learn the material very quickly. It's unlikely that you will be allocated much time to rehearse with your new colleagues unless you are a principal. Instead of a full-company dress rehearsal, you'll probably be given a blocking call so you know where you're going onstage and with whom, but the emphasis will very much be on you slotting into the ongoing perform-ances in the most seamless way possible. And you need to do this in such a way that your principal and ensemble col-leagues are not thrown off track. Bit by bit, you'll have the opportunity to develop a healthier interaction with your colleagues, but as the only new member of a well-oiled pro-duction, it will probably be helpful if you make your mark in a gradual way.

## Technical Rehearsals

Moving from the rehearsal room to the theatre is a mile-stone during any production – and a particular moment I love. It is the day when it all becomes real. For the last few weeks of rehearsals, the company will have been running the show in increasingly large chunks – scenes, whole acts, full runs – so by this stage, you and your fellow performers should have a firm grasp of your characters and the narra-tive of the entire piece. Dance routines will have been learned and perfected; musical numbers will be honed and primed for performance. You know exactly where and when you enter and exit, where to collect and return props, and which set pieces you'll need to manoeuvre on or around. But until you actually make that move into the theatre and get onto the set, you will not have truly tested any of your mate-rial in the actual space – and finding your feet there, although wonderfully exciting, can feel very different. Most importantly, the technical rehearsals are the time for that specialised team to slot everything carefully into place, plot scene changes, programme automation, orchestrate cos-tume changes, and map out lighting and sound cues.

Theatres, both new and old, have different personalities, dif-ferent boundaries and different dangers. Safety onstage and off becomes of paramount importance when you move onto the set. Most modern musicals are technologically very complicated, with large set pieces moving very quickly and, in some instances, weighing tons. Some stages revolve with small gaps in between each turning plate where toes and fingers could become trapped. Many stages have trapdoors opening onto stairwells, ladders or hydraulic lifts, whilst others are divided into smaller sections that morph during each scene change, with individual sections being lifted high above stage level or dropping away beneath it. Most shows will have set pieces that are flown onto stage quickly and flown back up into the flies even quicker. Older theatres often have limited space in the wings to store scenery while it is not being used, which means heavy scenic pieces are often strung and hung above your head. Lighting rigs and sound equipment will inevitably need to be manoeuvred and repositioned during technical rehearsals, and automated set trucks or pallets will be whizzing on and offstage into the wings.

Theatres can be hazardous places to work, but it's always amazing the level of care and attention to detail that technical theatre staff bring to their jobs. They take safety very seriously, as should you. Thankfully, in spite of the technical complexity of most modern productions, accidents are a relatively rare occurrence. Read the rules, listen to instructions, and stay alert. This is of great importance during the technical rehearsals where everything is new and everyone's stress is at its height. The technical rehearsals for *Miss Saigon* at the Theatre Royal Drury Lane were particularly complex. At the time, it was the most ambitious, technologically advanced and expensive musical ever mounted – and at times the stage could be quite frightening for the cast. When we looked up, the famous helicopter and a limousine dangled just above our heads. One poor girl got trapped between the huge statue of Ho Chi Minh and another piece of scenery when both gargantuan set pieces were moving. It was the devil's own job getting her out, but fortunately she wasn't hurt.

Technical rehearsals are the domain of the stage-management team, who are in charge of coordinating all the scene changes, making sure props and set pieces move on and offstage easily and safely, and that everyone is where they need to be at any time. These people will be the first point of contact between you and the creative team. Although they will be extremely busy, it's important that you communicate to them anything you think will ultimately not work or could be improved. Don't bother them with trifles, but technical rehearsals are the optimum time to iron out any serious problems. For safety's sake it's incredibly important you listen and respond quickly to everything they ask you to do.

Staying alert during technical rehearsals can often be a challenge, and many actors metaphorically 'drop the ball' of their own performance during this period. The theatre is often totally dark during techs, with only little pools of light in the auditorium, glowing from the workstations of the technical teams. It's a surreal environment in which to spend eight or more hours of your day, and there will inevitably be large chunks of time when you will not be needed. It can be very easy to allow yourself to get distracted by prolonged periods of chatter, lose your concentration, and begin to get on the nerves of those who are desperately trying to get work done. Instead, it's a perfect opportunity to run quietly through dialogue with other members of the company, but continue to stay limber and warm. Technical rehearsals will always last days and sometimes weeks, so make absolutely sure that the first complete run-through onstage is not the first time you've worked through your material since leaving the rehearsal studios.

Technical rehearsals have a tendency to create a certain amount of dust and debris inside theatres – many of which are very old – no matter how hard the people involved try to prevent it happening. However, if this floating detritus becomes obvious in the air, be aware that it can play havoc with your lungs and vocal cords. Avoid it where you can. Teams of people will be rushing in and out of doors and depending on the season, the theatre can also have extreme changes in temperature and humidity. It's all a recipe for a possible throat or chest infection. To keep in health, stay properly hydrated, dress warmly and get plenty of rest. If you are not required to be waiting in the wings or the stalls of the theatre, inform stage management of your whereabouts or wait in your dressing room.

It's also when you move into the theatre that your dressing room will be allocated and, if you want to share with a particular friend, you should apply to the company manager while still in the rehearsal room. If you're going into a show that is already up and running, you won't have this luxury; you'll be given the dressing room of the person you are replacing. Respect that space, whether you are sharing it or not.

### The sitzprobe

At some stage towards the end of technical rehearsals, you'll have what's called a sitzprobe – literally, the German for 'seated rehearsal' – where the cast and orchestra are integrated for the first time. Traditionally, the sitzprobe will take place in whatever space the orchestra has been rehearsing, and it is the first and most intimate interaction you will have with your colleagues from the orchestra pit.

It's a heart-stirring experience to hear the music in all its glory and empowered by live musicians. You will quickly see how the orchestra underpins and supports your material as well as the narrative of the whole piece. Relish the moment, because once the orchestra moves into the pit, you will not have the opportunity to sing so closely with them again. For weeks, you have been relying on piano accompaniment, and suddenly at the sitzprobe you have to find your note from an entire orchestra. If you are unhappy with something, you can ask to do it again but, unfortunately, there is not always time to repeat numbers. Musicians are expensive and are booked for a certain number of hours. If the rehearsal goes a minute over time, the producers face an additional fee, and for a large orchestra that means a considerable sum of money. Be prepared for the sitzprobe, stay firmly tuned to your conductor and the orchestra so your songs go as smoothly as possible.

The sitzprobe is unquestionably a time for celebration because it usually marks the beginning of the end of technical rehearsals and serves as the precursor for the final big push. All elements of the production will now come together very quickly and you will begin to start running longer sections of the show, if not complete acts, onstage with lighting, wigs, make-up, costumes and sound being added in significant portions. Opening night is right around the corner!

### The sound

Perhaps the biggest change – and challenge – you'll experience onstage during the final techs is the addition of amplified sound. As a performer, you'll now begin to wear a radio microphone, probably concealed in your hair or elsewhere, with a wire taped to your body leading to the transmitter/battery pack strapped round your waist.

Constructing a sound design is one of the most difficult and imperfect sciences in theatre, because a mix must be established between acoustic and amplified sound that enables the performers, the conductor and the orchestra to work seamlessly together. Add to that the need to create a sound product that will enhance the narrative of the story whilst satisfying and thrilling audiences, and you have a recipe for real headaches.

We have yet to witness the opening of a musical where sound does not become an issue for virtually everyone at some stage. All performers will want to hear more of themselves, or more or less of a particular instrument. Musicians will want to hear less of the stage, none of the sound effects and more of each other, so they can play together. The musical director wants and needs to hear everything. Some producers and directors will want to shake the theatre to its foundations, whilst others want to be able to hear a pin drop onstage. And the audience wants to get what it paid for. It is not an easy job, and virtually every sound designer has the skin of a rhinoceros – or a stomach ulcer.

Your job is to not panic and to be as patient as possible. Of course, you must let the sound department know what you need to perform best onstage, but always make sure you do it through appropriate channels and as politely as possible. Generally, the sound team will bend over backwards to help you, and are often some of the calmest people in the theatre to deal with – even when they're getting it in the neck from an insecure performer. Ultimately, you must understand that things won't sound as they did at the sitzprobe. You should show faith in the team that is working with you, as well as appreciate that this aspect of the production is one of the most complex conundrums to get right in live theatre performance. To make matters worse, everything changes once an audience is in attendance, changing the acoustics of the venue, and often a workable mix is not achieved until the very last second.

## The Dress Rehearsal

If the orchestra is large, the producers may have suddenly doubled their employment costs, so there is always real financial urgency for everyone to move as efficiently as possible towards the first preview and a paying public. Don't be surprised if you notice the tension levels of the creative team begin to escalate exponentially as the pressure mounts. Keep calm, don't pay too much attention or get involved in the inevitable maelstrom of madness that will be spinning all around you. You've got enough to be thinking about your part in the production, so try to let the pandemonium wash over you and stay on target.

Whether you're in a brand-new musical or taking over in one that is up and running, you will probably get just one dress rehearsal. This is the time when you well and truly discover not only how the entire show fits together, but how securely you know your character and the role it plays in the whole piece. It's the moment when everything should come together, from a technical, artistic, emotional and practical point of view. If it's a new show, you'll invariably move directly from a dress rehearsal into a first preview; if the show is already in production, you'll dive straight into the deep end of performing with an established company that is seasoned in performance.

Dress rehearsals are notorious for either being spectacularly smooth or absolutely catastrophic. Do not take either outcome too seriously; keep your mind on fundamentals at this stage and, most importantly, keep your eye on the finish line. Do not let anything or anyone distract you from achieving your perfect performance. Virtual tornadoes of activity by the creative and technical teams will thunder throughout the theatre, but you must keep your head when all about you seem to be losing theirs.

## Previews

The purpose of previews is to enable the creative and technical teams, along with the producers, to observe the show objectively and make any last-minute adjustments or corrections to the production prior to the show being reviewed by the press. The reality of making meaningful changes at this stage is debatable, but without doubt, many shows have been saved from ruination because of the revisions and refinements that have been implemented in these final days leading up to the opening night. The Broadway musical *Spider-Man: Turn Off the Dark* required a record preview period of 182 public performances until the producers felt it was ready to open officially.

Previews are a tough time, but there's something exhilarating about flying by the seat of your pants in this way. You will be rehearsing any revisions or refinements made by the creative team during the day, and then performing a slightly modified or 'improved' show each night until they feel it is absolutely spot on. This is another chance to speak up if you feel that something is not quite right. It's also the time to settle in to the piece, maybe experimenting just a little with your characterisation or tweaking certain moments, maybe your comic timing on a particular line, to get the reaction you and the director are seeking. Sometimes it's a good idea to invite a trusted friend or your agent to a preview, so you can receive some objective feedback from somebody not involved in the production.

Since tickets are generally a bit cheaper during previews, it is understood that the show is still a work in progress and can be stopped at any time if something goes badly wrong. Having said that, you must never work on that premise, but endeavour to deliver a professional, polished show that is worthy of an opening night, not just a preview. You never know who will be in the audience; there's a strong chance that online reviewers and bloggers will be watching, and they won't give you the benefit of the doubt just because it's a preview performance.

Your journey from the first day of rehearsals to this moment will have been nothing short of extraordinary. And now it's time for opening night...

'Razzle Dazzle'
Part Four: Performing

# 4

# Performing

## Opening Night

For actors, musicians, creative team and producers alike, opening night is an electrifying occasion. Family, friends, colleagues, special guests, and the paying public will all be in attendance, wishing you and the show a fabulous and successful night. With each opening night there's an inescapable buzz in the air, and everyone is desperate to experience something brilliant and completely out of the ordinary. Of course, the critics will also be in the audience, and this is the night that your beloved show will unquestionably be subjected to their sometimes enthusiastic, sometimes frosty and unforgiving glare.

As soon as you walk through the stage door on the day of your opening night, there's a sense of optimism and anticipation that sparks off everybody and everything. Final rehearsals will be taking place onstage; messages and gifts will be given and received; your dressing room will look like a cross between a greetings-card store and a florist's shop; the odd bottle of bubbly will be stashed waiting, hopefully, for a triumphant moment to be uncorked. Right up to the stage manager's call for beginners to take their places, cast members, crew and directors will be knocking on doors to say 'Break a leg!', 'Merde!' or 'Toi toi toi!' – all backstage ways of saying 'Good luck!' (which is itself rarely said because it is still thought by some to threaten the exact opposite). The adrenalin levels will be rising to peak intensity, and the toilets will be in constant use, sometimes by those who just need a few minutes alone to ease the tension of the build-up to the big event.

When that Act One Beginners' call is finally broadcast over the tannoy, there will a collective backstage dash into position. Hearing the overture, stepping onto the stage and, at long last, facing the responsibility and the rapture of playing your character in front of an audience is sensational. First opening night or last, principal performer or ensemble member, an opening night becomes a colourful milestone in your life, ever to be remembered. Regardless of whether the success of the night lies partly or largely in your hands, you will always be aware that it has taken the entire cast, crew and orchestra to make it work. A show, hit or failure, you will quickly understand, is a showbiz family affair.

It's easy to be swept up by the fever of this entire day, but essential that you stay focused on your target and not get carried away by the creative buzz of it all. Opening nights can feel terribly momentous, frantic and sometimes a bit crazy, but your job is to remain faithful to your role and your direction. Never lose sight of what you have been asked to do, concentrate on creating a performance that consolidates all those fierce weeks of rehearsal, and don't let the mad excitement of the occasion persuade you to step out of character for a second. Stay on course and, one way or another, the night will be yours.

The very best opening nights end with the audience leaping to their feet with pleasure – and the critics rushing away to write their reviews. But no matter how wonderful the applause, everything will be eclipsed by the overwhelming sense of satisfaction in knowing that, collectively, your new theatrical family has conjured up an evening of sheer magic. Star names rarely make a show a success on their own. It's teamwork and unbending attention to detail that makes that magic.

The producers will probably lay on a party after the show, usually an opportunity to hobnob with a few big names from the entertainment world, and at which you can celebrate for a few hours with the cast – and maybe a few members of your real family too, if you're allowed to invite them. It's a marvellous release from any secret worries and stress that have probably been building up through the weeks of very hard graft. You've earned the chance to let your hair down, but don't go too mad – there's another performance the next day and another audience expecting to see you at your most scintillating. Don't overdo it!

## Your Theatre Family

Although I have a wonderful and loving family, the theatre has always been a second home to me. And it's when you start the regular performances of a show that this sense of a theatre family really comes to the fore. Once in the theatre, you will be surrounded every night by lots of people from the various departments: lighting and sound, wardrobe and wigs, dressers and stagehands, front-of-house staff, theatre managers and musicians, as well as your fellow actors. You will be living and working with them, cheek by jowl, eight shows a week, and probably spending more time together than you do with your partner, friends or family combined.

The theatre virtually becomes your new home and it makes sense to invest time in forming good relationships. Politeness and consideration for everyone will go a long way towards a smooth-running show. The smart thing is to take the view that no one person is more important than any other; everyone matters in making the whole production work well. Besides, when a two-ton piece of set is flying past your head or you're nearly naked in the wings trying to get into costume to make your next scene, it's always reassuring to know someone's 'got your back'.

Company managers are the mum or dad of the show, the bridge between the performers and the producers. Their job is part-pastoral, and they look after you in all sorts of ways.

They'll come round the dressing rooms to let you know everything that is going on, hand out the payslips, help you book tickets for friends, and sort out any problems that crop up. They're brilliant at understanding people, so don't bottle anything up. Small and large problems alike, the company manager will deal with them. Incidentally, in straight plays the company manager may also be the stage manager, but in musicals, this is rarely the case because the responsibilities for both positions are so diverse.

There are other members of your theatre family, and it is very worthwhile developing good relationships with them. The stage-door keeper is there to give you your dressing-room key and your post, to take messages for you, and to let you know when you have a guest. Theirs is the first and last face you will see each day. Your dresser is there to help you get ready for the show, as well as assist you in your costume changes. Work closely with them and tell them what you need. When I'm in a new show, there's one particular dresser I always request, not only because she's so good, but because she also understands how I work, warts and all. One show required a complete change of costume in thirty-four seconds; something I initially thought impossible. But my dresser and I persisted, created our own choreography for the change and, with flawless teamwork, we did it every time. Dressers are not lackeys there to run errands for you and they are not paid a great deal, so it's considered good manners to tip them. Ask the wardrobe mistress or a colleague for advice on what that amount should be if it's your first time.

### The Press

Throughout your performing career, the press is liable to make its presence felt and it's a fair bet that you won't like everything the critics say about what you do onstage. A number of them have been reviewing a long time and they take their jobs very seriously, so you have to learn to cope with criticism when it comes. It pays, however, to be guarded in what you do and say outside the theatre, because some newspapers and their readers seem to thrive on gossip – and, in these days of technical gadgetry and mobile-phone cameras, nothing seems to stay secret for very long.

Theatre criticism carries with it a great deal of power for the simple reason that quite a lot of people are influenced by what is written or broadcast. But ultimately, as we are aware, it is often the public deciding what succeeds and what fails. Nevertheless, when the critics get it wrong, it can be disastrous and, at the very least, unnecessarily hurtful. It is a complex and unpredictable interplay between the critics, the performers and the audience. It is also, incidentally, the theme of one of the West End and Broadway's most successful shows, Mel Brooks's *The Producers*.

Reviewers are human, too, and their opinions can be based on all manner of things. When *Crazy for You* opened in the West End, it received brilliant reviews, numerous awards, and tickets were like gold dust. My leading man was Kirby Ward, an old-fashioned song-and-dance man, handsome, charming and a fantastic rhythmical mover with shades of Donald O'Connor, Gene Kelly's wonderful comedic dance partner in the movie *Singin' in the Rain*. Kirby was a good actor and singer – and an absolutely brilliant dance partner. To the inch, I knew exactly how hard he would spin me, precisely where his outstretched hand would be at any given moment and his lifts were effortlessly perfect. We moved as one, and yet the critic of one of the UK's biggest national newspapers took a dislike to him. When I later confronted the writer – a lovely, sharp-witted man who later became a friend – and asked why he was so disparaging about Kirby's performance, he said the dancer reminded him of the comedian Tommy Trinder from years ago, who had fronted the big TV show *Sunday Night at the London Palladium*. He had disliked Trinder intensely and that had affected his view of Kirby's portrayal. He admitted that he had not been as objective or fair as he should have been about my leading man. It didn't affect the success of the show in any way and Kirby laughed it off, but, deep down, I knew he was very puzzled and hurt by it.

When Leonard Bernstein started conducting the New York Philharmonic after World War Two, he was branded a self-indulgent, hedonistic fake by one American critic, who hated his work and remained ruthlessly against the composer throughout his career. Bernstein ignored him and left us a legacy of genius. Who remembers the critic?

With the rapid proliferation of online message-boards, Facebook, Twitter, and the rise in the number of self-appointed critics writing blogs, the traditional media outlets are not alone these days. Although sometimes very well informed (and no one should ever totally disregard another's opinions anyway), the judgements from all the 'new' critics are subjective, personal, and possibly distorted by the writer's special prejudices. I am far from convinced that it is smart to get involved in social-media battles with them when they are rude or disparaging. But I suppose it's always tempting to say thanks for compliments!

*Les Misérables* is the perfect example of the critics being ignored by the public. It received abominable reviews when it first opened in London: 'a witless and synthetic entertainment,' said one critic; another dubbed it 'The Glums'. Today, more than twenty-five years later, with the show still wowing audiences in the West End, *Les Mis* continues on its marvellous musical way. Cameron Mackintosh displays those awful reviews in his Bedford Square office in London as an important reminder to be answerable only to the public, and not the whims of critics. It's what happens at the box office that counts, and *Les Mis* proved, in the most extraordinary way, that there is nothing more powerful than word of mouth.

Not every show you'll be in will be liked by the critics, and not every critic will like you. You'll have to find your own way of dealing with any brickbats and flak, as well as enjoying the moments of praise. But that's easier said than done. Over the years, I have been delighted by good reviews and devastated by negative ones, so now I don't read any of them. Lots of performers are the same, believing there's some truth in the old adage that if you believe the good reviews, you've got to believe the bad ones too. I prefer the opinions of the director, my trusted friends and family (who are surprisingly honest!).

Avoiding reviews may not work for everyone – and it's true that you will still pick up on the general tone of what the critics have said by the general buzz about the show, comments from friends, and the billboards outside the theatre – but I find that actively devouring reviews the morning after an opening night is a stress I'm very happy to have left behind. For the same reasons, I don't go searching for myself online or on social-networking sites. Those who do must be prepared to face the full gamut of often very personal, unfair reactions, even downright defamation, as well as praise and, as I said earlier, trying to fight your corner on these networks may prove unproductive and more trouble than it's worth.

## Anxiety and Nerves

Getting nervous is completely normal – especially on opening nights, when you're about to set off on the most terrifying, stomach-churning roller-coaster. Here's the good and the bad news: it gets easier, but it never goes away entirely. The reality of facing hundreds, sometimes thousands, of audience members (not to mention the critics) can disconcert the most experienced of performers. Laurence Olivier famously wrote in his autobiography of struggling with performance anxiety throughout his whole career.

After forgetting lyrics to a song in a 1967 concert, Barbra Streisand was unable to perform in public for close to three decades. There is no question that adrenalin can help sharpen the mind and quicken reactions in performance, but only up to a point. When butterflies or jitters become outright stage fright, it's important to tackle it head-on and look carefully at exactly why it's happening and how to diminish it.

Like many performers, I have a vision of accomplishment against which I constantly measure myself. High standards must be maintained, but it is dangerous to have too many thoughts or feelings that you are not hitting your best. This can lead to performance depression. An unrealistic refusal by some performers to accept anything short of an idealised view of perfection has been known to create a self-destructive cycle of worry and, sometimes, real illness and failure. Long-term psychological harm can result from constantly measuring yourself against standards that are not always attainable. It can slowly sap self-confidence and lead on to anxiety and then fear. I know because I've seen it happen to a couple of people.

Giving your best will rarely get you into problems, but some psychologists believe that the creative process itself can trigger anxiety. Simply put, being creative as a performer is well and truly about stepping outside comfort zones and taking risks, in the rehearsal room as well as in front of large audiences. Nerves in our business are natural and I've met very few actors who don't suffer from them in some form. They can even sometimes give an extra edge to a portrayal and I can assure you that most times, once the music starts and you are on, you are so busy doing your thing that the nerves fly away. Until the next time!

Here are some strategies for tackling that anxiety and nervousness:

- If you make a mistake, forget your words, crack a note, trip or tumble over the furniture onstage, you need to recognise that we are all human and capable of falling on our backsides. Don't worry about making a fool of yourself. We all do it, we all blunder once in a while and when it happens you have to laugh, learn and move on.

- Try pinning all your energies on the task in front of you to the exclusion of everything else. Certainly, don't get self-conscious about the audience or a desire to make them 'love' you. Push all other thoughts out of your mind apart from your material and how you are going play your part. It's easier than you think and, when you've found the knack of doing it, you'll go a long way towards establishing a healthy, confident mind-set for the future.

- Before stepping onto stage, think only of your first scene and nothing else. Target each moment as it occurs. Do not brood over the entirety of the piece or the scale of everything you must remember and execute. Trust in your preparation and concentrate on each piece as it occurs. Don't ruminate over the next, possibly more difficult scene, or you might just forget the one you're in. If a concert pianist were to mull over every note he must remember in a Beethoven concerto before performing, he'd never venture onstage. Hours of training and rehearsing have led you to this moment; your body and brain will know what to do as the show unfolds, but take it step by step.

It's so important when tackling stage fright to remember that we humans are capable of achieving great performances, but never perfect ones. It's only through our mistakes that we learn to work better and grow wiser. The secret is to embrace your fears. The adrenalin racing through your body is telling you that you're tackling your ambitions and achieving your goals. You can usually expect your nerves to disappear as you get into the production's run. If they don't and they get in the way, seek advice.

## Settling In

The thrill of opening night is soon supplanted with the relief that comes after the main creative team disappear, and you finally have the time and space to let your performance breathe a bit, without the constant scrutiny and note-giving of your directors and producers. Now that you are into the run of the production, real opportunities exist to explore and experiment with your character and your performance.

In the UK, resident directors are usually entrusted with the day-to-day preservation of the creative team's ideas; in the US, the production stage manager bears that responsibility. Part of their role is to enable you to grow and evolve in your role, and the best of them will be as keen as you to find fresh nuances in your part. Of course, they are also there to rein you in if you stray too far, but generally speaking they will encourage you to advance your understanding of the character and support your endeavours to mature in the role.

Providing your fellow cast members are growing and developing their performances alongside you, it can be a crucial period in your own blossoming as a performer. Inevitably, you will come across some colleagues who will prefer to act and sing their part more or less the same way from opening to closing night, but, where you can, you should seek out those colleagues who will challenge and stimulate your own flowering as an artist. Acting is so much more exciting when you work with people who refuse to repeat a performance night after night, and who will truly search for innovation and spontaneity.

I'm not suggesting for one minute that you should be desperately seeking to change the way that you and the director have agreed you will play the part. It is just that ideas will often occur instinctively, and repressing those impulses can actually be counterproductive to the honesty of the moment. Simple things – like a new inflection in the voice, an altered movement, look or gesture, or a new-found moment of stillness – can keep things alive and fresh for you onstage. It is important to stay truthful to each moment as it comes – you are always aiming to *be*, not to demonstrate, your character – and sometimes that requires a certain degree of flexibility and daring. Theatre magic often comes from taking risks and sometimes it's artistically necessary to follow your most instinctive impulses, even if it means sometimes getting it wrong. Don't ever be afraid of looking silly! I repeat – we've all been there a time or two.

Besides, part of the excitement for an audience is the knowledge that no two nights are ever exactly the same. Anything can and does happen in live performances and there will always be differences from one night to another in the way an actor turns a phrase or sings a song. There's an uncertainty and spontaneity about live theatre that is so beguiling and keeps people coming back for more, especially in contrast to the often-predictable, multimedia-blitzed age in which we live.

## Audiences

Audiences themselves have a role to play in each performance. They are not merely consumers. Each audience has a personality of its own, and its sensitivity and responsiveness can profoundly influence the dynamism and shape of any given performance. Sometimes a few enthusiastic punters will infect the rest of an audience with the volume of their applause or the size and style of their laughter. The resultant atmosphere throughout the evening will be very fluid and interactive between audience and cast. American audiences often seem to fall into this category, intuitively wanting to encourage the actors onstage through their appreciation and applause. Conversely, a shy but attentive audience may watch and listen intensely throughout the night, not wanting to interfere in any way with the performance, and then erupt at the end with a rapturous ovation. British audiences can often behave in this way.

The audiences that sit in silence and don't applaud at the moments when you hoped they would are the ones you perhaps need to pay the most attention to. When that happens, it might be time for the resident director to schedule some emergency rehearsals and for the company to pull their collective socks up. It's impossible to judge how an audience will respond from one night to the next, but there's no question that they have a participatory presence. Ultimately, their impact on our performances, and vice versa, is theatrical voodoo; it's part of what makes live theatre so compelling and exciting.

## Performance Protocol

### Calls

Before each show begins, there are a series of checks and balances that must take place to ensure the smooth running of the subsequent performance, and it's important for you to know the professional etiquette expected of you at this time. This pre-performance protocol may vary depending on where you're performing and, maybe, the different rules and regulations in each territory, but certain things are globally applicable.

Every show on every continent will have a half-hour call before curtain. This means that thirty minutes before the performance begins you must inform stage management that you are present and physically in the theatre. Informing stage management usually comprises of 'signing in', which means ticking a box on a list at stage door, or sometimes signing your signature. Do not be persuaded to sign-in on the behalf of friends. This is a recipe for real trouble and could potentially have a profound impact on the performance should your colleague be further detained or delayed.

Stage management will religiously inspect the sign-in sheet at the half-hour call and, if people are not present, under-studies and swings will be called into action to cover any absentees. Some roles may require an excessive amount of pre-performance preparation in terms of make-up, wigs or costumes. As Elphaba in *Wicked* or the title character in *Phantom of the Opera*, for instance, you'd have an earlier call because of the green or deformed facial make-up those characters wear, and the longer time it will take to apply it.

Some shows insist on a mandatory warm-up; others may require brief but consistent rehearsals prior to performance to ensure that dangerous fight scenes, staging or choreogra-phy is being executed safely. In these instances, you may have a forty-five-minute or an hour call prior to curtain and, again, it's essential you arrive when required. Those calls are put in place by the creative team and company management for your physical health and safety, as well as the needs of the show.

The half hour leading up to the beginning of any perform-ance can be chaotic. A complex stage-management schedule will be put into place, carefully routing actors to the sound department to get miked up. Along with this, wardrobe, wigs and make-up are all busy, ensuring that everyone gets the help and assistance they require in order to be ready in time. You must stick like glue to the timetable because, if you are late, it will have a knock-on effect for the other people assisting you, and for your colleagues. Punctuality is expected, as well as being good manners.

## Warm-ups

Whatever sort of production you're in – straight play, musical or opera – if there is not a compulsory company warm-up, it's a matter of some importance to your long-term professional well-being that you physically and vocally warm yourself up – and you should be doing this prior to your half-hour call and not after. Complications and, sometimes, emergencies can spring up after the half-hour call, and if you fail to warm up adequately before then, you may find yourself in a situation where you're having to dance or sing without having adequately prepared your body and voice.

In long runs, there are many times when you will be tired, perhaps unwell and less than enthusiastic about going on, but the constancy and routine of warm-ups will do wonders in strengthening your resolve and ability to pull through these tough periods. Performing cold is unprofessional, often results in injuries and is unfair to those you work with – and the audience. Having a specific time and space allocated for actors to warm up freely is hugely beneficial to all, and can really bring a company together onstage and off.

When I was in *Putting It Together* on Broadway, warm-ups became a ritual to look forward to, and they always ended in a cast hug. It's foolish not to acknowledge that a bit of pre-performance camaraderie can really contribute to keeping a cast healthy, happy and right up to the mark. Unfortunately, not all managements agree. Where mandatory warm-ups are not the norm, you should seize responsibility for keeping your own body, voice and mind warm and well-tuned.

The backstage area in most theatres is usually pretty cramped and everyone needs their own space. If you are thinking of using your half-hour call to go through every scale and arpeggio under the sun in full voice, or stretching into the splits right in the way of gangway traffic, think again – or you'll soon have no friends left in the building. Any warm-ups you do after the half-hour call, whether vocal or physical, should be as brief and as private as possible so as not to intrude on your colleagues. They've got their part of the business to look after.

## Final calls

After stage management confirms that all actors are physically present in the theatre, you must stay there until after the show is finished. Managements disapprove of actors in full make-up and wigs having a chat or cigarette outside the stage door. More importantly, they need to know that they can communicate to you over the tannoy system prior to curtain should any emergency occur.

The fifteen-minute call will be the next one you'll receive, and you should be well into your preparation by this stage. Again, it's another marker for you to use in establishing a consistent and safe routine prior to curtain. Your last chance is the five-minute call, but you really should be completely ready to go by this stage. You might get into the habit of using those final five minutes for a gentle warm-up or a quiet moment to think yourself into what you are about to do. Finally, you will hear 'Act One Beginners to the stage!' or 'Places!' This is when you must move swiftly into your starting position, and ensure stage management know you are there. Then, you're off…!

## Performance Behaviour: the Good, the Bad and the Ugly

Inhabiting a character onstage takes an immense amount of concentration. There has to be an element of almost stopping the clock and losing yourself entirely in a different reality. In order to stay in that state of total focus, you need like-minded colleagues to play against. There is no greater hardship than having to act a scene with someone who is the artistic equivalent of a cosmic black hole, absorbing everything you give without ever giving anything back. Your reputation is your greatest asset as a performer – and you will gain a good one by staying totally committed, generous and responsive onstage.

It's tempting for young actors new to the business to want to fit in, to be 'one of the gang', but beware of doing this at the expense of your professionalism and pride. Our business is attractive to, and couldn't do without, people who are uninhibited and colourfully liberated of mind, but there are sometimes one or two who are just as interested in having fun as making art. They are who they are, invariably great company and possibly very talented, but their career trajectory will almost always reflect their priorities. If you want to be taken seriously in this business, the single-minded, passionate route is the only one. This advice is not just for principals, but for absolutely everyone involved in the show. The principals will have their moments, but you must never lose sight of the truth that some of the best parts in lots of productions are the lovely, natural interactions between ensemble characters that an audience sees as authentic and wonderfully enjoyable. Regardless of the size or importance of your role and your level of responsibility to the production, live for those moments and be respectful of your craft and colleagues at all times.

I am not suggesting you have got to be a po-faced party pooper to make it in musical theatre. Far from it. It's a business that fizzes with charisma, fire and energy – and it mostly attracts young people with those qualities. We all need to laugh and let off steam once in a while. It's just a question of how and when you do it. I've never forgotten that Judi Dench, a noted practical joker, once said in an interview that our job is important because it can change someone's day, lift people's spirits – but we are not saving lives like a surgeon. In other words, we have to find a good balance in our private and professional lives, and how we get our kicks.

## Being a leader

We don't always feel a million dollars, but never underestimate the influence your mood and attitude has on your colleagues at work. Leave your troubles at the stage door and don't carry any sulks into the dressing room. Low spirits and bad temper can spread into a company, affecting life onstage and off. If you're a leading man or leading lady, it is so important that you set a high behaviour bar for yourself, a benchmark for the entire company. Like it or not, your actions and conduct will be constantly scrutinised by everybody involved in the show. How you handle yourself and others can hugely affect the tone of the entire building. Good humour and civility are wonderfully contagious and uplifting.

The success of the show is the responsibility of everybody in it, and if someone constantly performs poorly in your estimation, misbehaves or is impacting adversely on the cast with their behaviour, it is right to do something about it. Do not take it upon yourself to become the director and give out advice or admonishment; that is not your job or prerogative. Always go through the resident director, production stage manager or company manager, where the problem can be discussed objectively and calmly. It is their responsibility to decide what action needs to be taken. Taking things into your own hands can lead to all sorts of extra troubles.

Be generous with your fellow actors and they will usually reciprocate. Many directors use the metaphor of one actor passing an imaginary ball to another to help describe the importance of passing focus to whoever is speaking onstage. It is very rude to upstage another member of cast by drawing attention to yourself when the attention should clearly be on them. I was guilty of this once in *A Chorus Line*, not out of big-headedness or self-importance, but because I thought it added to the humour of the show. One of the characters, Connie Wong, is supposed to get the attention in the tap number because she is so bad at it. I discovered I could get a laugh by imitating her disastrous efforts whilst she was performing. The choreographer quickly put a stop to it, pointing out that Connie needed to emphasise her own inadequacies for the sake of the story. I meant well but it was thoughtless to the show and to my colleague.

## Corpsing

'Corpsing' is theatre slang for laughing or causing others to laugh out of character whilst onstage. Some say the term originated from the temptation to try and provoke laughter from an actor playing a corpse onstage. Amusing, funny things do happen out of the blue during a performance and it is often hard, sometimes impossible, not to laugh. Imagine for a moment the strain on an actor playing a corpse, trying to lie absolutely still, not moving a muscle. If something occurs that the other actors find amusing, the pressure can build up further and further until it reaches a point where it's finally got to blow. The release valve is the laughter itself and when the awful moment comes there is often no way of stopping it.

Most of us are prone to getting the giggles, often at the most inopportune times and in the worst circumstances, and it really is very hard to hold them back. You will very likely be involved in corpsing at some stage in your career, either the cause of it or as a result of someone else's words or actions. A friend said that when it happened to him in a murder mystery, he thought his head would explode because he was bursting to laugh, but also terrified because it would undoubtedly wreck the scene. He pulled some frightful faces, then sat with his head in his hands whilst apparently considering some aspect of the case. He managed, just, to win through.

John Barrowman is a man of many talents: singer, dancer, actor, television presenter and reality-show judge. He's proof positive that no one needs to accept being pigeonholed in this business. I absolutely adore him, but he's notoriously naughty, a frightful corpser, and he gave me an awful time one night while we were appearing together in the Stephen Sondheim revue *Putting It Together*. We had a very sexy dance number called 'Bang!', and right at the most sultry bit of our choreography, John split his pants practically in two. A frantic bit of emergency repair with duct tape took place in the wings before our next duet, 'Unworthy of Your Love', but we had the most terrible time keeping our giggles at bay throughout that song. John was just as naughty when we appeared in the television series *The Sound of Musicals*, as the many out-takes can attest, but all the silliness can ultimately be swept under the carpet on television by re-recording until you get it right. You can't do that onstage.

If somebody starts to corpse or fool about when a principal is in the heart of their big song or scene, causing him or her to falter, that person is going to be in a heap of trouble, not only with the lead actor, but with management and producers alike. The offender will need to go immediately on bended knee to all and apologise profusely. Even if the principal continues flawlessly, it puts an added and unwelcome burden on their performance and the transgression will no doubt result in a serious dressing-down, if not from the singer personally, then certainly somebody with real clout.

### Messing around

Corpsing is in some instances unavoidable, but quite wrong if it stems from performers messing around. In a pantomime, this laughter can be very infectious and spread over the footlights into the audience. Actually, it is often preplanned and rehearsed for exactly this effect. But when the joke comes from actors deliberately teasing and provoking others into laughter onstage, it can have a sour effect on the audience. If performers are sharing a private laugh out of character, one instinct of the audience will be to think that the joke is on them. To feel excluded from a joke is never a nice feeling, whether it occurs in a school playground or at work. Audiences lay out a lot of money for theatre seats these days and have every right to feel short-changed if treated in a cavalier fashion. On the other hand, audiences are frequently amused and understanding when something untoward happens spontaneously or accidentally onstage and produces laughter in quite the wrong place.

During a performance of *Chicago*, way back when Michael Grandage was its resident director, for some inane reason I started surreptitiously, as I thought, tickling some of the cast. He didn't see this thoughtless stupidity, but friends of his who were in that night told him what I'd done. As fans of mine too, they were very disappointed in me; they said it looked as if I didn't care. Michael told me this plainly, sadly, without anger, but it really hit me hard. Rightly, as the leading lady, I felt utterly humiliated.

## Going wrong

We are all aware of the description 'showstopper': the song or performance that generates such rapturous applause from the audience that everything comes to a halt onstage. Everyone wants to deliver one of those! But the moments where things go wrong so badly that the action is stopped and the cast, technical team and orchestra must start again are perhaps one of the most mortifying experiences a performer can ever face. Generally, when things go wrong you have to just grit your teeth, carry on, and hope the audience won't notice – and most times they don't. Sometimes, however, there's no other option but to stop the show, literally.

In *She Loves Me*, I had a fast, tricky number called 'Where's My Shoe?' Wearing pyjamas, I had to rush around the room seizing things to wear while the leading man, played by John

Gordon Sinclair, stands by, protesting that he is not going to tell their boss that she's not really ill. I had sung it dozens of times without a hitch, but in this one particular show, I somehow entered at the wrong point in the music and then couldn't find my way back into the correct place in the song. The audience was clearly aware of the mistake. At that moment, I felt that there was only one thing I could do. So I stopped the orchestra, put the props back into place, and started again. The audience was thoroughly amused by it, but afterwards I remember wanting the ground to open up and swallow me whole. Gordy realised that there was no way back and helped me through it as if mesmerised by the entire hilarious occurrence. He said afterwards he thought it was brilliant and brave – and has dined out on the story ever since.

Audiences appreciate that things may go wrong in previews, but they weren't expecting what happened at the first preview of *Putting It Together*. One of my numbers in the show was an amusing, pacey song called 'More' (originally written for the movie *Dick Tracy*), which I danced with a small bag, a huge feather boa and jewels, whilst attempting a tongue-twisting middle section at breakneck speed. On my first public performance I got myself into such a muddle with it that I simply stopped the show and proclaimed to the audience that I had just experienced a 'brain fart'. I started again, got it perfect and the audience went wild with applause. There was some sense of satisfaction that I got through the moment, but I was nonetheless very upset with myself. No sooner did I get into the wings than I ran straight into the show's composer, Stephen Sondheim, and its producer, Cameron Mackintosh. They'd been sitting in the audience and witnessed the whole debacle; Stephen smiled, hugged me and said well done for dealing with it in the way that I did, adding, 'But don't do it again!' He told me how another leading lady had done a similar thing in one of his other shows and been so intoxicated by the rapturous reception she received that she faked the same problem every night until Stephen found out and put a stop to it. I told him I had no desire to repeat the exercise.

It's not just tongue-twisting lyrics that can unintentionally stop a show, but wardrobe malfunctions too. When *Putting It Together* was being filmed for American television, Carol Burnett's skirt brought proceedings to a total halt. It slipped down, bit by bit, inch by inch and, as it finally fell to the floor, she threw up her arms as if to say, 'Surprise!' The entire audience erupted with laughter and it was impossible to continue for a long time. The whole comic event was captured by the film company that produced a DVD of the show, and appears at the end of it as an out-take.

Being prepared for the unpredictable is part of the fun. When I was new to playing Nancy in *Oliver!*, I noticed a small trickle of water worryingly running down the centre of the stage heading toward the orchestra pit. As I tracked the liquid path upstage, it seemed to seep out from Fagin's large chest of props. I reported this potential hazard to stage management – was there perhaps a dangerous leak under the stage? – and I was told, to my horror, that this was the chest into which the young boys playing Fagin's gang of urchins occasionally hopped in order to relieve themselves, having ignored constant entreaties by their chaperones to spend a penny before the curtain went up. The glamour of the stage takes many forms, but you'll never be short of laughs. Just save them for your dressing room!

## Publicity

Just because the musical you're in is on a theatre's billboard and has received some advance press, it doesn't mean that audiences will come automatically. The show may be one of lots of musicals currently playing and costing hundreds of thousands of pounds, or dollars, a week to keep running.

The owners must promote, advertise and sell their product; and as a member of the cast, you are part of that product.

If you're playing a principal role, you will undoubtedly be asked very early on to assist in the publicity and marketing of the musical. It may well mean giving up some of your precious spare time, but it's worth bearing in mind that this sort of activity can give both you and the show a boost. Your willingness to cooperate and help sell tickets will hold you in good stead with both producers and the media.

If you are asked to be interviewed by television, radio or the press, it's good to remember the five Ws: who, what, where, when and why. The press will want to know:

- *Who* are the creators and directors and *who* is in the cast?

- *What* is the show about and *what* part do you play in it?

- *Where* is the show playing and *when* does it open?

- *Why* should audiences spend their hard-earned cash and come to see it? Spell out one or two particularly attractive points in the musical.

Rattle off these answers and you'll survive virtually any publicity interview. Always stick to the facts and never make claims that cannot be validated or substantiated. Keep answers short and concise, and endeavour to use language that the majority of readers or viewers will understand. Some producers will have publicity departments that will advise you on what they do and do not want you to say in the course of your interview; after all, they don't want you to give away all their secrets and surprises.

Whenever I have moved into a new role I have been closely involved with publicising the musical, talking to any number of showbiz writers and struggling out of bed early enough to appear – and to sing – on several TV breakfast shows, sometimes on the morning of opening night, but more often spread across a week or so before it. You don't often get an orchestra on breakfast television, and finding the high notes with just a piano at 7.30 a.m. when you would normally be asleep is not always so easy. Almost without exception, I have found press and TV interviewers helpful and charming, and there's clear evidence that exercises like this are very valuable in whetting the public appetite and putting bums on seats.

We have to recognise, especially after first nights, that not every word in newspapers and magazines, or comments on radio and television will necessarily be favourable to what we are trying to achieve. The critics have a job to do and must do it as they see fit, but the media can also be powerful allies and we need all the backing we can get in this business. I have to say that throughout my career – through a bit of light-hearted prince-dating, marriage, children and divorce – I have found that if you are straight with the media, they are generally pretty square with you. That said, it is always smart to pick your words with care, bearing in mind that once something has been said and is in print, it is in the public domain for ever, and can be used to your advantage, or against it, at any later stage.

Although principals will do the lion's share of publicity, all members of the company will be expected to get involved in promoting the show when asked. This may mean full-company appearances on television (such as *Children in Need* or *Good Morning America*), particular events (West End Live, West End Eurovision or Broadway Bares), and via their own Facebook and Twitter accounts. Many musicals in the West End and on Broadway have thrived into long-running life because their widespread fan base has generated excited word of mouth and created a buzz around the whole thing. If you use Facebook and Twitter, you can be proactive about the show, but never say anything that will undermine or embarrass your colleagues or the production. If you do, you might appear in the press in a way that would be rather less than helpful. Today's newspapers are full of stories about people who have opened their mouth too wide online, and put their foot in it.

## Sustaining a Long Run

Sometimes the run of a musical is intentionally limited – or, unfortunately, cut prematurely short by the production closing early. At these times, casts are often absolutely on their toes and inspired each time they face an audience, in the hope, perhaps, that the show will move on elsewhere or that some way can be found to save it. But it's a different matter keeping that energy at top level when you're doing eight shows a week for months on end. For starters, the demands on your body and voice are many.

The voice is a clever and responsive thing, if treated with respect. While I was in *Miss Saigon*, the director wanted a particular note sung in a chesty voice to find the sound he thought right for that moment of emotion. With care, I learned how to mix the head and the chest voices, so I did not strain myself, and it worked well.

As mentioned earlier, performing in *Marguerite*, I got into real vocal trouble. Following the emotional turmoil of my sister's death, and playing an unremitting, demanding role in the end took its toll on both my body and voice. I had sadly lost sight of the importance of maintaining good physical fitness and vocal health during this period – but it's particularly at these times, when we are stressed or depressed, that we need this regime to sustain us. I hadn't kept up with my lessons and now needed help, so I sought the assistance of voice coach, Paul Farringdon. Paul immediately understood that the demands of the show combined with my overwhelming personal sadness had seriously derailed my voice. He told me that what I was experiencing was much more common than I realised and he gave me a completely new routine of sensible, regular vocal practice. Through this careful work, combined with rest, Paul was thankfully able to reboot my voice. He also made me promise not to wait that long again before checking in with him or another voice specialist.

During a long run, you should have your voice checked to make sure you're doing things correctly. Try and make it something as regular as a car's MOT. If you think there is something amiss, don't just hope it will sort itself out. It might not and this can mean, as in my case, time in voice rehab to fix the problem. If singing is your career, voice specialists are a necessity, not a luxury. Look after your voice because, in certain cases, there may be no easy solution – or even no way back at all.

Take the odd class on your days off to keep your fitness and develop new skills, but don't overstretch yourself when you're performing every evening (and twice on matinee days). If it's a two-and-a-half-hour show, that might mean being onstage for up to twenty hours a week, spread over six days. Maintaining good physical fitness levels will also increase your confidence and mood. Good psychological health is as important as anything else in voice production because it enables you to produce sound with a fully relaxed and assured instrument: your body. Additionally, exercise is brilliant in helping clear airways of excess mucus, increasing lung capacity and strengthening breath control.

Drink adequate amounts of water and stay properly hydrated to ensure glands are functioning properly and vocal folds remain moist. Two litres of water each day is recommended. Vocal folds need to be lubricated with a thin, clear layer of mucus in order to vibrate efficiently, but if you regularly suffer from too much mucus production and it's interfering with your vocal fluidity, lower your intake of casein (the protein in milk or cheese) and the gluten in bread. Caffeine and alcohol cause dehydration and starve your vocal folds of much-needed lubrication. Smoking tobacco or marijuana irritates the entire vocal tract, has adverse effects on the heart and lungs and is certainly less than helpful to a singer.

The air inside theatres can become extremely dry, with air conditioners, radiators or gas furnaces sometimes contributing towards a harsh working environment for singers. Using a humidifier to get more moisture into your dressing-room air, as well as one at home, makes a lot of sense. When you're flying somewhere by plane, the atmospheric differences and artificial air conditions of the cabin can also cause problems with vocal cords. You should keep yourself well hydrated and, of course, refuse all complimentary alcoholic beverages!

Loud throat-clearing or harsh coughing should be avoided. They are usually an indication of either a thick coating on the cords, due to dehydration; or too much mucus from a cold or, possibly, an allergic reaction to certain foods. They can really have quite an impact on your voice's health, especially if the vocal cords are already suffering from inflammation. Avoid yelling and regularly try and reduce the demands you make on your voice by resting it completely. When you have to speak, do so with as little effort and tension as possible, and always make sure you breathe properly before articulating a sentence or a lyric. Just as vocal warm-ups are crucial to good singing health, so are vocal warm-downs. After any strenuous performance, always allocate a few minutes of time to gently siren up and down the scales to recalibrate your vocal folds. It may all seem overly fussy, but these are paramount considerations when your voice is your livelihood.

Prescription drugs can affect the way you sing, and it is always best to check with your doctor or chemist to determine if something you are taking might impact adversely on your voice. Over-the-counter antihistamines, for instance, are notorious for causing dryness, and a local anaesthetic you might take for a sore throat can sometimes be counterproductive. It may not be the sort of treatment too many young musical-theatre hopefuls are rushing in to, but Botox injections anywhere in the head region are infamous for causing vocal-cord difficulties in singers. Some birth-control pills that are progesterone-dominant can affect the larynx and decrease the upper range. Acid reflux (where acid from the stomach flows back into the oesophagus) is a very real danger to vocal cords and if you suffer regularly with it, you should immediately discuss ways of controlling it with your doctor.

Adequate rest is perhaps as important as anything in maintaining good vocal health, so make sure you get the right amount of sleep. For some, celebrating with colleagues and friends at the end of an adrenalin-fuelled performance seems the instinctive way to wind down and relax, but try not to have too many late nights on the trot.

Ultimately, the more you look after your body and your talents, the better you will be able to sustain your performance in a long-running show. If you're performing well, you're more likely to have that contract renewed and stand in better stead for a longer-lasting career overall. Be good to yourself, have as many check-ups with your singing teacher as you can afford, and see your doctor for a regular overhaul. A good balance of physical health and bright spirits is the thing to aim for.

Some of this may appear obvious and unnecessary, even elementary, but you will notice already how often I have fallen short of my own rules and expectations over the years. Sometimes it was accidental, sometimes my own silly fault, but ours really is a job like no other. We're lucky to be doing something that is so enjoyable for ourselves and for others, so it makes sense to have a workable regime that sustains what we do. Unfortunately, everybody gets ill sometimes, but bear in mind that, when you're in a show and can't perform for whatever reason, chances are you won't get paid. Somebody else has to do your specialised job. Your attitude and sharp attention to detail is what oils a successful performing career.

## Saying Goodbye

The length of time you stay in a long-running show is often a matter of circumstances and choice. Most contracts in the UK last for one year because that is generally the period over which the producers hope to recoup their investment and they don't want the added expense of recasting and re-rehearsing within that first year. I have usually found that twelve months in a show is about right. That's when the feeling creeps in that it's time to look for another job – but it will vary from production to production for all manner of reasons: conditions, status, resources, personal and professional.

There are at least two shows that, for various reasons, I have performed in for more than that one-year contract. When I was in *Cats*, I stayed with the show for the better part of two years, because I was understudying so many roles, and relishing the variety night after night. I also enjoyed performing with a wonderful company. None of us were yet well known, and fans seeking autographs at the stage door would have to ask us for our names because we were so unrecognisable out of the cat make-up we wore onstage. I have also had a long relationship with the Kander and Ebb musical *Chicago*, returning to the two leading roles of Roxie Hart and Velma Kelly several times, and on both sides of the Atlantic. Both are such compelling characters that I've always found more to explore each time I've gone back in to the show.

I absolutely loved performing in *Crazy for You*, especially as it was my first starring role in the West End, and it was a difficult decision to leave the show. But after a year, Kirby Ward was going back to America, and I couldn't face the idea of dancing with anybody else. It's desperately hard to leave a role you have created, feel that you own and one that has given you a thrilling, successful time, but sometimes you need to be brave and leave on a high. It was just as well I did in that case, too, because *She Loves Me* came along almost immediately.

The length of time that feels right for one performer might be entirely different for another, and you need to be aware of your capacity to commit completely over an extended period. Quite a lot of people have the temperament to stay in a long-running production and continue to give great performances, but some actors, having explored every aspect of the character they can, may feel it becoming a chore. If you tire of it and can't give it one hundred per cent every night, as the audience has paid for and deserves to see, then it's time to leave. It's one of the reasons directors like to bring in a new face or two every so often: it helps freshen the whole thing up.

It's not possible to forecast when you will feel it is the right time to move on so, when and where possible, you should ensure your agent negotiates a reasonable get-out clause with the producers. Ideally, you'd want the contractual flexibility to quit when you feel you can no longer give your best to the show. Equally, should a new project arise that you want to take on, having the option to leave when it suits you best is always the ideal position to be in – but in practice, this sort of arrangement is not always easy to come by.

## Getting Your Notice

At some stage in your career, you'll almost certainly experience being given notice by the producers. It's one of the toughest and saddest things for any company to face.

Generally, everyone is called to the stage by the producers and told that the show will be closing on a certain date for whatever reason – usually because audiences have stopped coming. When I was in *Peggy Sue Got Married*, word of mouth was starting to build a good audience, but then came 9/11. The world was in shock and worried about where the next blow might fall. International tourism came to an abrupt halt and many people just stopped going to the theatre. Feel-good musicals especially felt the draught. *Peggy Sue* deserved a longer run but, along with one or two other shows, was forced to close.

However long you may have anticipated the arrival of this moment, the reality of being told you will be out of work on a specific date, maybe months before you expected it, is always painful and daunting. You, your fellow performers, the crew and orchestra have dedicated yourselves to the production and it is very upsetting to realise that the public is no longer responding to your blood, sweat and tears. But everybody in theatre must learn to live with this threat. There are legendary tales of musicals that, following savage reviews and poor advance sales, have closed after a calamitously short time. It happened to Alan Jay Lerner, librettist and lyricist for the blockbuster musical and movie, *My Fair Lady*. His last show, *Dance a Little Closer*, closed after just one performance. Today in the West End, however, you must be given at least two weeks' notice of a show's closure. Even so, it's not long to find that you're out of a job. The unpredictable lifespan of a show, along with the ephemeral, fluctuating appetite of the theatregoing public, are sensible reasons why you should try and save some money when you are earning.

Unless the show gets a reprieve – it sometimes happens if bookings start to pick up again – or there is a national tour planned in which you're offered a role, you must begin the search for something else. Preparing for new auditions will be your first priority and, for this reason, even when you have the 'security' of a year's contract, you should always be thinking about expanding and practising your repertoire. In fact, when you're *in* work is exactly the right time to be doing this. If and when notice is given – and no show lasts for ever – it can be some consolation to know that you feel geared up for a fresh challenge.

When the final performance comes, it is very often an emotional experience. Naturally it will feel somewhat heightened, but treat it as you have done throughout the run – with the same level of energy, spirit and commitment. You may have performed these scenes and these songs several hundred times, but you'll never do so again – at least not with this company, in these circumstances. Make the most of it and it is likely to be memorable, with lots of fans of the production in attendance and showing support.

Occasionally, a penultimate performance is sometimes played as a 'muck-up matinee', where the cast deliberately change some of the lyrics or play little tricks on one another. If you must do it, make sure the audience doesn't see it. They may not feel this is what they paid for.

And then it's all over. You hang up your costume for the last time, take down the good-luck cards, pack up your things, and say goodbye to cast and crew, your dresser, the stage-door keeper. You may have spent many wonderful months with this extended family, performing a show you love, and it's always difficult coming to terms with the fact that it's not going to last for ever. Post-show blues are part of the life of a performer. But this is not an ending; it's a new beginning. Another job, another family, a new set of experiences, are waiting round the corner…

'Nice Work If You Can Get It'
Part Five: Working

# 5

# Working

The excitement of rehearsing and the exhilaration of per-forming are what has brought you into musical theatre. But unless you're in work, then life as a performer can become demoralising and difficult. If you are still training, have recently graduated, or have even been in the business for many years, you will need to spend time developing your career and how you go about getting work. Drama schools and training courses will give you good advice on finding that sometimes elusive first job when you step out into the pro-fession, but you must also think for yourself about the career you want to forge, and the people you want to support you.

## Getting Started

Regardless of the course you've completed, graduation is both a moment of elation and trepidation. Taking this step into the theatrical world is a terrific thrill but there are still plenty of challenges to face – not least finding an agent. Some lucky and talented people may have been spotted and found one before graduation, but most students will enter this stage alone – sometimes in more ways than one.

The contest for work is beginning and it's a race you'll be running for the rest of your working life. Very little in our business comes easily and those that succeed are usually the ones who have fought the hardest and persevered the longest. Talent is vital, but it will only get you work when combined with sheer determination, ambition and as much of a plan as you can muster at this stage of the game.

There are people in the business who will state quite boldly that what graduates have achieved thus far is a product and that, like all new products, it now has to be marketed and sold. I don't like this description, it's too impersonal and totally loses sight of the heart and soul that young performers pour into what they do. But the fact remains that you do have something to sell – and you're the one who is going to have to do most of the selling. In the early days anyway, you may feel pretty much alone in the driving seat.

A good place to start is by analysing exactly what it is you bring to the theatre, and how it is different, perhaps unique, compared with what others have to offer. The world is your oyster as long as you have a realistic view of the world you are moving in to. The real question you must answer is 'What am *I* going to add to this overcrowded business, brimming with talented artists, that will be distinctive and irresistible, and how best can I let people know about it?'

If you start your professional life with the vague and easy thought of 'I must now find an agent, attend auditions and get a job,' you could be casting yourself out to sea with no engine and no sail. Preferably before you leave drama school, you should formulate a 'business plan' for your career, or at least part of one. If you have already left drama school, or even left some time ago, then there is no harm in taking stock of where you are now, and what you still want to achieve in the future.

### Your 'Business Plan'

As you're reading this, you may well be saying, 'I'm an artist, not a businessman/woman… That's why I need an agent. It's *their* job to find me work.' But that can be a very narrow-minded attitude. Your agent will contribute to finding work for you – submitting you for auditions, introducing you to important contacts, negotiating your contracts, and so on –

but they cannot get you the job. That is something only you can do. Without doubt, an agent is going to be an important part of your team, but they are not the be-all and end-all. You should not be discouraged if you are not recruited by one before or straight after you leave your training.

In any case, you should actively want to take charge of your own success, rather than relying entirely on someone else. The American columnist Lewis Grizzard wrote, 'Life is like a dogsled team. If you ain't the lead dog, the scenery never changes.' Not everybody is destined to be lead dog, but you can be the leader in your own life, instead of allowing your fate to rest completely in the hands of others.

I know that, like most of us at this stage, you will be pleased to be offered pretty much any job to get your career started. But, until something comes up, it does no harm to think through everything you've achieved, re-establish just what your special skills are, how you see your future in the business, and what extra help you can drum up to achieve this. For the young performer, the sky is always the limit – and that's as it should be. Until you get out there and start competing for the jobs, you will have only a limited idea of just how hot the competition may be and how far you might go. However, this is a good time to be sure you make the most of who you are – and who you know.

If you're lucky, tutors, lecturers, coaches and choreographers at college or drama school will have pulled in all sorts of people from musical theatre to help with your training and to talk to you – I've done a number of workshops and talks of this nature – and it may well be that you have impressed one or two of them. It's the nature of the beast to try and get noticed on these occasions. If you hear or read that any of these people are involved with something you think you are suited to, make certain you get to the audition or, if there isn't one, try and contact that person and remind them that they saw you sing, dance or whatever. You never know when the miracle will work and your face will fit. It's happened before and it will happen again; after all, it's new, talented performers that help make the musical theatre world go round.

It's also worth remembering that although you are basically on your own, there are quite a lot of people who want to see you succeed, quite apart from your family. Teachers, mentors, vocal coaches, dance instructors, and other influences you have now left behind, still have an interest in seeing you do well. If you need advice, you should not be afraid to call on any of them for help. It's a feather in their cap when you make good.

There are a lot of simple but essential questions to ask yourself early on. Are you a brilliant dancer who can sing and act, or are you a great actor who can move and sing well? What are your strengths? What physical characteristics do you have and how can they best be used? What special things can you bring to the stage? And what 'research and development' are you prepared to carry out? In other words, are you going to make the effort yourself to find work and discover what roles are on offer at any given time – or are you going to wait and leave it all up to your agent?

You need to be realistic about where you'll fit into the profession, and will no doubt have consulted with mentors and coaches to get their views on what areas of the business you are best suited to – although you should have pretty clear ideas of your own as well. Hopefully, it will also have been pointed out to you the sort of competition you face and what you will need to do to make your mark, the little tricks of the trade that will pick you out as exceptional. For instance, if the field you aspire to enter is full of good actors, but few can dance as well as you, that is something you should exploit. Find a way of making sure the people running the audition or interview are aware of all your strengths. One important extra skill can often make all the difference.

You will have to get used to the idea that, maybe all your working life, you will have to find ways of kind of advertising and promoting yourself. You must ensure that the people who matter in theatre don't lose sight of you. They need to know that you are the sort of professional who is not afraid of a challenge and will do your utmost in all circumstances.

An increasing number of performers, many well-known, use social-networking opportunities (Facebook, Twitter and so on) for this purpose today, and there's no doubt they are a great way of disseminating whatever news it is you want to spread. Personally, I have some reservations about how this form of communication should be used – which we'll come back to later in this chapter.

## Agents

Most drama colleges and schools send their students out into the world of work after final-year, full-scale musical productions, often led by professional directors and chore-ographers, followed by a showcase at the end of the term for graduating students. The school will invite agents to attend, as well as proud parents, family and friends – and often the general public too.

Drama schools attract leading agents to their productions and showcases and, in some instances, directors who have a new project in mind and are looking for a fresh face. These end-of-year shows are extremely important because you will be hoping to be picked up as a result of an outstanding performance. Not everyone succeeds in this, and it can be a fraught experience if some of your friends and fellow students get offers of representation from agents and you don't. It's not necessarily because they performed better, but often because those particular agents have people with similar talents and looks as you already on their books. It's a hard business, and knocks of this nature are frequent. Be confident in what you do, and carry on until you find someone who recognises your particular talents and who feels he or she can help you find work.

Regardless of whether or not you come up trumps with an agent at the end of your training, finding the right one for you will be one of the most fundamental decisions of your professional life and is not something to rush into. Indeed, for most, it's impossible to rush, because most agents tend to be pretty choosy. They will take on only those young artists they feel have something special they can sell. Conversely, it's important that you decide on an agent that can actually see and identify the complete range of your talents; one who has the experience and connections to exploit your particular abilities. Finding an agent who has the same attitude as you is the kind of partnership you should seek.

You can search for agents online or using *Contacts*, a vital resource that features, as the name suggests, lists of contacts across all areas of the entertainment industry. Do your research before approaching agencies. Some will specialise in dance clients, others in drama. Some have a very diverse list and will do a bit of everything: musical theatre, television, film, commercials, voice-overs. With a bit of research, you can usually find the client lists of any particular agency online and, from that list, you can garner a pretty accurate view of whether or not this is an agency that is likely to be interested in you. In an ideal world, it's best to find an agent that has no one else like you on his or her books. Not necessarily easy, but you don't really want to be competing at auditions with other clients from the same agency. Indeed, being unique to that prospective agency can be one of the most compelling arguments you can make in offering yourself to them as a potential client.

When deciding on which agents to meet, try to seek out someone who is properly interested in finding out who you are and what you can do. It's vital you choose an agent who is not only professional and honest, but one who understands you as a performer and will put you forward for the jobs you stand a good chance of getting, not just anything and everything under the sun. Smaller agencies can sometimes provide a rookie performer with a more personalised relationship and might be more motivated to get you working as soon as possible, whereas a larger firm will not be depending on your income for their survival. On the other hand, some larger agencies will have links in the industry that are long-established and well-respected, and this can often be pivotal in which direction your career takes. Both have advantages and disadvantages that you must weigh up carefully when making a final choice.

Whatever decision you ultimately make, this is a business partnership and you need to keep it that way. Be cautious about becoming too friendly with your agent. As much as you may get to like one another, it's best that the relationship remain on a business level so when difficult circumstances arrive – as they quite often do – you can both look at them objectively. At many different stages of your career you will need unbiased and rational advice – most especially from your agent – and that could be made much more difficult if you are mates. Equally, if the time does come to sever the business relationship between you, hopefully it can be done professionally and swiftly, so both parties can move on.

Good agents will try and find as many opportunities as possible for you to meet directors and casting directors, or indeed anybody who could potentially be helpful. These opportunities will probably consist of simple introductions and not necessarily lunches at The Ivy! It's all about putting you into as many minds as possible, so it doesn't matter whether there's a job going or not. Seize any opportunity to speak to the movers and shakers in the business. You'll be pleasantly surprised by their interest, because, after all, the one thing they're all seeking is brilliant new talent. Be self-assured without being pushy. Let them know what you can do and leave a good impression. Theatre people, especially directors, are good networkers, and frequently pass on information when one of their colleagues is looking for someone new. The wider your contacts, the better your chances.

Some agents still operate at the 'old rate' of ten per cent, but most will now take twelve-and-a-half per cent of your earnings. Before ever signing a contract with an agent, read it over a number times so you understand exactly what the relationship is you're forming with them. Take it very seriously because it could have profound implications at a later date. If there are clauses that you don't understand, ask for clarification. Your new agent must understand that you are taking the contract just as seriously, as they most certainly will should any conflict arise between either party. The most common dispute between agent and client comes when somebody chooses to leave an agency. You are liable to pay your agent their commission for any job they submitted you for, regardless of whether or not you have left their agency. If possible, run the contract by a solicitor or a trustworthy third party to gain any objective observations on its content and fairness.

Ultimately, agents can pick and choose who they want as clients but, once a business relationship is formed, they are there to work with you and for you. Any good business relationship must be built on mutual respect, understanding and trust, but you are called a 'client' for a reason. Your agent is paid by you to market and promote you; if, over time, they fail to do that effectively, then it may be time to consider bringing that relationship to a close and finding somebody who will look after you better. Equally, any good agent will expect new clients to be motivated, professional, punctual and determined. If you fail to demonstrate those qualities, he or she could be the one deciding to end the relationship.

## Contracts

Once you have an agent, it will be their responsibility to negotiate the terms of your contracts when you are offered a job. This should always be the result of a two-way conversation in which you can outline your hopes and expectations, and they can advise on the finer points of the contract. Remember that contracts are enforceable by law – so if you don't understand something, ask! It's good to always read through your contracts carefully and get used to making your way through the legal jargon. Many performers at the start of their careers have little understanding of the legal implications of signing a contract and simply audition for anything and everything, regardless of whether or not they can actually take the job if offered it. However, taking an audition for employment that you cannot accept can be a dangerous idea.

My first professional job was working a summer season at the seaside; not quite the end-of-the-pier playhouse, but very close to it! A good talent-spotter and happy with my work, the producer persuaded me to sign a contract early for the subsequent summer season. In my guileless ignorance, I assumed that if something better cropped up, they would let me go. Sure enough, the following year, auditions were being held for a new production of *A Chorus Line*. Up at dawn and first in the queue at the audition, I sang and danced my way into the show. But the production was touring at exactly the time I had my obligation to the seaside summer season, and the producer wasn't budging, insisting – as was his right – that I honour the contract.

A little bit of luck and a lot of innocence were on my side in that particular instance. The *Chorus Line* team allowed me to start the tour, break for the summer season, fulfilling my contractual obligations there, and then finish the tour. But I had allowed a complicated scenario to unravel, which no one appreciated in the end. Thankfully it all worked out, but

I upset several people along the way, to such an extent that I was nearly sent on my way from *A Chorus Line*, my biggest break at that time.

Learn from my lesson, and understand that when you take an audition, you are essentially saying to potential employers that you are willing and able to accept that job, should it be offered. Turning down an offer because contract negotiations over terms or money have gone wrong is very different to turning down a job offer because you were not available in the first place. Be careful not to waste the time and money of people who are capable of offering you work. They may have long memories.

## Managers

Managers usually come into their own with clients who have already begun to make their mark in the industry, so most newcomers to the business will not normally need one. Traditionally, a manager will take an intimate interest in promoting, cultivating and marketing their clients; and often guide financial decisions as well as help manage income. Consequently, they work in a very personal way with their clients, advising on every aspect of their career and, for this reason, look after a smaller number than an agent would. The best of them will have the experience and influence to turn a career full of potential into one of attainment and accolades. Most mangers charge a fifteen to twenty per cent commission for the work they're involved in, which would be an additional sum on top of your agent's commission for your acting work.

Commissions to both an agent and a manager are a hefty responsibility. It's not something you want to consider, therefore, until you begin to achieve and earn at a level that warrants this kind of personalised service. Increasingly, some managers are taking on the responsibilities of agents, especially in the area of submitting their clients for castings. There is no doubt that in recent years the distinction between agents and managers has blurred a bit, but ultimately, you want someone who understands your talent, cares about you as a person and as a professional, and can negotiate the best deals on your behalf.

## Coaches and Classes

When you're training, it's easy to take for granted the resources and opportunities at your disposal. Your career starts while you're still at drama school, not after you graduate. So make the most of the multiple opportunities you have while still there. Secure real allies for the future in both your fellow students and your instructors. Many of the staff teaching in drama schools in the UK also work in, or are connected to, the musical-theatre industry. Final-year shows in particular are often directed, musically directed and choreographed by professionals. Most assuredly, the reputation and relationships you establish in school will follow you and can hugely influence the start of your career. All these people are part of your winning team and you may still need their assistance at some time, so make sure you keep them on side.

Once you graduate from drama school, unless you find immediate employment as a performer, all the skills and artistry that you've worked so hard to attain will be unused and wasted, unless you create a specific programme for yourself. It's not easy and it can also be expensive. What was always freely accessible (and free) to you as a student – the regular vocal tutoring, dance and acting classes – is no longer available to you in the same way. Therefore, you must exploit any and every contact you have to stay active and engaged in your own special techniques.

You have always got to be on top form in every way because you never know when something is going to come up;

sometimes it will be at very short notice. When you have a new number to learn at speed, you will need someone to play the piano for you and maybe help you develop your performance. Likewise, you might need a bit of coaching advice when you have a new monologue to tackle or dance steps to learn. Vocal coaches and dance classes can be expensive, but if you established good relationships with the experts at drama school you could have the odd ally to call on in an emergency. One girl I know cleaned the house of her singing teacher in exchange for lessons. If you have been collaborative and worked your socks off in their classes, former tutors have been known to help out because, as I say, any success you achieve will reflect on them. But they won't do it for ever – you are no longer paying the tuition fees!

## Photographers and Headshots

Without doubt, you will need good photographs that not only do you justice, but are stylistically up to date and relevant to the theatre industry. Headshots are a vital part of any actor's professional arsenal and something worth investing the right amount of time and money into getting right. Your headshot will be the first thing to hit the desks of casting directors and agents, and it needs to create an impression. It can have a lot to do with securing your first opportunity or audition.

Your headshot is not a job for the mobile-phone camera or for a friend with the latest expensive Nikon camera. Professional photographers don't come cheap, but these first pictures of you may just be the most important ones you ever have taken. What defines a great headshot? First and foremost, it needs to bring out your personality and not just the smart technical skills of the person taking it. You, the performer, are being unveiled, so every decision your photographer makes should be about revealing as much of you as possible rather than achieving some slick, archetypal facsimile.

There is a critical difference between creating a headshot that satisfies professional conventions and one that actually sparks off the page. It is something that takes real artistry on the part of the photographer to achieve, and something, you'll find, that is also quite rare. If you take any theatre programmes you may have tucked away and line up all of the actors' headshots side by side, you'll find your eye will be instinctively drawn to perhaps one or two photos at best. The others will just be photos. The ones that caught your eye will have transmitted a thought, feeling or strong streak of personality off the printed page. You need pictures that are going to find your character and catch the eye. They need to be of a competitive high quality, and look like you today and not some time ago. Photos that have been airbrushed or Photoshopped to create film-star or matinee-idol looks are an immediate turn-off for casting directors and agents alike. Often, the more tampering a photographer does to get the shot to look 'right', the less 'right' it looks.

Most performers have several facets to their talent, so why not have headshots that mirror that diversity? Besides, every casting is different and it stands to reason that if you can tailor your headshot to individual castings, you stand a better chance of securing that audition. Most headshot sessions are built around a specified number of 'looks', but not only a change of clothing – we're talking about a change of character. Typically, you can have the option of a 'three-look session' or a 'five-look session' (guess which costs you more money). If you choose one of these options, you should think long and hard about what types of roles you are most suited to play, and you might need to discuss and confirm your own ideas with individuals qualified to look at you objectively and professionally. Then take your choice of 'looks' from there. During a five-look session you might want to try and capture something on the lines of the following examples:

- Virile/beautiful, impassioned leading actor
- Casual, confident young performer
- Intelligent and thoughtful actor
- Contented and happy young parent
- Carefree and successful businessperson

Obviously, each of the above would require clothes to support and inform each character change, but more importantly you and your photographer have to communicate and collaborate to capture the right tone and feeling. One good headshot is better than five bad ones, but if you can afford it, different headshots for different submissions is the best bet.

A typical photo-shoot will generally take a full morning or afternoon in the studio, but make sure you check the price before you book. Studio time with a theatre-specific photographer can cost an arm and a leg, but is worth every penny if the pictures open doors and win jobs. Getting recommendations from friends and colleagues, your teachers or your agent is a smart idea, but you can also use the performers' bible *Contacts* or search online. Once you've shortlisted several photographers, schedule interviews with each. You can always look at their portfolios online, but it's vital that you meet each of them in person to determine which one you feel most comfortable with. Easy communication between you and a mutual understanding of what you want to achieve in your session will lead to a better overall photo-shoot. For women in particular, if possible, try and organise to have a hair and/or make-up professional attend the shoot with you. If you wish, take some music to help you relax or create a mood.

Colour headshots instead of black-and-white are now the norm. Unlike black-and-white photos, colour headshots allow casting directors and agents to discern eye and hair colour as well as skin tone. Almost all photographers now shoot digitally and the deciding powers will not care or, in most instances, be able to tell whether or not your photos were captured digitally or on film. The difference between the two is almost insignificant and the ease of digital photography makes the probability of capturing that one fantastic shot all the greater. Expect a typical shoot to produce in the region of four hundred pictures. Digital photography makes organising and editing the photos easy, so you should be able to pick out the best fairly quickly.

## Social Media

The social media is here to stay and, as we are all aware, the world and his wife, including many big names in the entertainment business, spend a lot of time posting messages to all and sundry on Facebook or Twitter. It can be a lot of fun, it can be informative and, maybe, used with sense and care, helpful to young hopefuls in musical theatre by getting your name known and extending your contacts. You could certainly let a lot of people know when you get that first marvellous stage job, where and when you are appearing, and how you feel about it all.

Used in the right way, the internet and social media can be a useful marketing tool, and we should all strive to understand how they work to harness their potential. It pays to be a real person since, if you concentrate on being friendly with other real people, sooner or later they'll check out what talents and skills you have to offer. These could be ties that have an affect on your career because it is yet another way of finding out what's going on in the business – and there are plenty of directors using the system.

A smart move is to become part of creating a community of like-minded artists and performers, all aiming for excellence and, maybe, opportunities to collaborate. You can certainly swap tales about your experiences so far, the people who have influenced you, your favourite shows, and so on. It can take some time, though syndicating the content across all different platforms and networks will speed up the job.

Never forget, however, that social media is very public and can be extremely unforgiving. Don't use it to let off steam, complain about colleagues or bad-mouth anything or anybody. Nobody likes a whinger. Likewise, be aware that not everybody is going to love you all the time or be permanently on your side. We read in our newspapers and see on our television screens, with sad regularity, the vicious effect the so-called trolls can have on innocent people. You have to bear in mind that there will always be people out there, full of jealousy, dissatisfaction or general bile, who get a kick out of hurting others and will seize every opportunity to put you down.

Faced with these, don't rise to any unfavourable comments that might be made by others about you; there are plenty of people ready to tear you down in the vilest fashion, all delivered anonymously, of course. Dignified silence is invariably the best policy. There was a high-profile example of one West End performer who took exception to a comment made about her on Twitter. Her subsequent retort to the member of the public made the news – and it was the performer who was portrayed as being aggressive and unreasonable.

Websites for individual performers are now the norm and should act as the centre for all of your additional social media. People will make judgements on the quality and content of your website, so it pays real dividends to invest in creating one that is worthy of you. You can either employ a web designer (though they can be expensive), or use one of the many website or software packages that enable a DIY approach. Keep it clear and classy and you'll go a long way towards communicating who you are as a performer, and how passionate you are about your profession.

## Developing Your Career

Until you make the right connection and sign with an agent, don't waste any time. Find ways of promoting yourself and looking for work on your own. You can send your CV and headshot to casting directors. You should look out for open auditions advertised in *The Stage*. You may want to subscribe to PCR (Production and Casting Report), a weekly casting bulletin, or one of the many online jobs services. You might feel it a good idea to continue some of these things even when you find an agent.

Always make sure your CV is up to date and accurate. Don't try to pad it out with things you think will sound impressive; and always be honest. The theatre world is smaller than you might think and very tuned-in. If you get found out over a silly lie (and some people have), it is embarrassing to say the least and not a good career move. Do include in your CV anything that you think might be relevant: any amateur work you've done, college plays, concerts, choirs, etc. After all, no one is expecting you to have a litany of professional work at this stage of your career, so what you've done as a student is completely relevant. Don't forget to have your current mobile number clearly printed on your CV because when things happen, they can happen quickly. You can also upload your photos and CV onto various websites, such as Casting Call Pro.

Go for everything you know you can do. You'll be learning valuable lessons with each new experience, as well as how to handle yourself and deal with other professionals. Above all, you need to be seen – so be brave. The fringe – in London, Edinburgh and around the UK – can offer excellent oppor-tunities to keep performing, work with other like-minded young professionals, and, just maybe, get seen. 'Profit share' rarely means that, though, because there is so rarely any profit. More often than not, it means that you'll be working for free.

There's nothing to stop you also going for jobs that you may feel are a bit out of your range because it's always important to keep challenging yourself and stepping out of your comfort zone. With each new opportunity, you'll be picking up tips and valuable insights into your craft. You'll be letting people know you are on the circuit and determined to succeed. Keep believing that one day the spotlight will fall on you – and chances are it will.

## Developing Your Craft

This chapter has so far been largely about the business side of the profession, because it's vital that you understand these aspects of your work in order to plan and develop your career to best advantage. But, as you deal with the necessities of contracts, casting and coaching, it is your craft that must remain in your heart and your mind.

One of the great challenges and gifts of being a performer is that the duty of maturing and growing as an artist is never-ending. Stretching the boundaries of our talent – as well as continually nurturing and developing skills – must be at the very core of everything we do. When you're training, keeping your eyes on growth and progress is easy, but entering the workplace brings different challenges. For a start, you have to sustain yourself financially and you must consciously carve out a schedule that enables you to continue to develop your talents while also trying to find work.

When you do win your first job, it's a great chance to take your career up a level. If you are in a full-scale, professional musical, suddenly you will be performing eight shows a week – probably more performances in one week than you have experienced in an entire year of your educational life. You will be working with other talented people and it's a fair bet that many of them will have vastly more experience than yourself and have much to teach you.

Each performance will bring opportunities to observe and assimilate alternative approaches and techniques as well as, hopefully, exploring and testing your own skills. Your first professional job should be a time for you to make an exponential leap in your own accomplishments, and the smart ones do not allow this opportunity to pass them by. Foolish newcomers – and I've known a few – are happy to tread water throughout the entirety of their contract and don't do much to improve their future career prospects. There is so much to pick up working with others. Learning from colleagues is perhaps the most valuable postgraduate course one could ever hope to have. Look and listen and you will be amazed how much you can grow in a short time.

In a business widely assumed to be filled by super-egos, I have frequently found the big names to be the most generous with their time and advice. The actor, director (and father of TV presenter Fern) Tony Britton took me under his wing on many occasions when I was rehearsing *The Sisterhood* at Chichester Festival Theatre. He told me, 'Being in musical theatre doesn't mean you can't act. Step up and take your place! Think about how you want to play this part and not just how we [the directors] think it should be played.' It was a wonderful, confidence-inspiring lesson about taking ownership of a part. During the same production, the assistant director (and son of Sir Peter) Edward Hall mentioned to me that he felt I was being gently manipulated by one of the senior members of the cast in terms of my position onstage. When the actor tried it again, I felt strong enough to say, 'No, that doesn't work for me,' and immediately heard Ed exhaling a rapturous 'Y-e-e-e-e-s'. Some lessons – like standing your ground, or taking ownership of your decisions – can only be learnt when you're working.

I returned to Chichester a few years later to play the lead in *Divorce Me, Darling!*, Sandy Wilson's sequel to *The Boy Friend*. The cast had over thirty members, with many well-known musical-theatre names (including Rosemarie Ford, Tim Flavin, Marti Webb, Andrew Halliday and Linzi Hately). But I learnt most from watching close-up the work of Joan Savage and Jack Tripp, both wonderful revue and panto performers, and the incomparable Liliane Montevecchi, a seventy-one-year-old French bombshell and former member of the Folies Bergère. Her sultry song 'Blondes are for Danger' was the highlight of the show for many critics, but I never minded because performing alongside her was like attending a masterclass.

Of all the lessons I have learned from colleagues, I will never forget Jim Dale's professional attitude when playing Fagin in *Oliver!* He was always doing something to lift the role, with no two performances the same. It was electrifying playing Nancy opposite him. During the run, Jim suffered a close family bereavement, but would not take a break from the show. He felt that stopping work would only give him more time to think about his tragic loss, which he couldn't bear. There is something to be said for putting on the mask of a character, going out onstage, and losing yourself for a couple of hours. It's not possible to think of anything else. Staying with the show was also a wonderfully unselfish act towards the rest of the company and the paying audience. Jim didn't miss a single performance.

## Beyond Musicals

Although you may have trained specifically for musical theatre, never be afraid to branch out into other areas of the entertainment industry if the right opportunities arise. Sometimes the only way forward is to take a step to the side first. If you feel you can tackle a new challenge, take it. Straight plays, television, cabaret, voice-overs, performing on cruise ships or in a band will all teach you valuable lessons about performance. You might have the opportunity to perform in concerts – either solo ones or in concert performances of musicals – and make albums – again, either solo or original cast recordings. The more diverse the opportunities you embrace, the better rounded you will become as a performer.

In fact, staying open to new experiences and being ready to snap them up when they occur is a huge part of surviving long-term in this industry. It's impossible to predict how one bit of work may lead to another, but it's a certainty that work generally leads to more work as you widen your sphere of contacts and colleagues. Overanalysis of your career and your opportunities can sometimes lead to a kind of paralysis, so keep a certain amount of cheery optimism and gung-ho openness.

Sometimes when you come to a fork in the road, you have to take it and see where it will lead – listen to 'The Road You Didn't Take' from Stephen Sondheim's *Follies*! Of course, it's crucial to re-evaluate career choices, but it's equally important to trust your instincts and allow each experience and opportunity to unfold and develop. Sometimes the detours can be more interesting than the main route.

## Non-musical theatre

You would think that acting in plays without songs – usually referred to as 'straight theatre' – is the easiest step for musical-theatre performers to make; certainly easier than television and other mediums. Yet many theatre directors still harbour an outdated bias towards actors who come from a musical background. You'll need to persevere and believe that if you're good enough to get the work, one day you will get it. Your training will most certainly prepare you to do any kind of live theatrical work, and adding non-musical theatre to your list of credits is a worthy and potentially pivotal goal to pursue.

I left the role of Ellen in *Miss Saigon* to play the mouthy maid in *Valentine's Day*, a musical version of George

Bernard Shaw's play *You Never Can Tell*, which premiered in Chichester. Suddenly, a whole succession of roles – all as servants – unfolded for me, and I was cast as a maid in Shakespeare's *Henry VIII* in the same Chichester season. Tony Britton, playing the monarch, told the director that I was a 'refugee' from musical theatre, and I quickly found myself being asked to sing a sixteenth-century ballad during the production, my one and only Shakespearean performance. The director had a rather fearsome reputation for being tough, traditional and unswerving in his attitude to performing the Bard, so this was a kind gesture to a relative newcomer to the industry, and a total newcomer to Shakespeare. You really never can tell what will happen.

When I performed in West End revival of Noël Coward's *Blithe Spirit*, I was reminded of the dramatic differences between a musical and a play, particularly regarding the pace on and offstage. In a musical, if you are not onstage, you are rushing to and from costume changes, switching shoes, having your radio mic adjusted, rushing to the loo, warming up, all the while accompanied by the non-stop, exhilarating force of the orchestra over the backstage tannoy. In *Blithe Spirit*, we performed the play at a cracking lick too, but the on and offstage energy required was serene compared to the velocity and dynamism of a musical. It was a much more laid-back experience: gentle, warm and stimulating. With only two or three people onstage at any given time, the sort of energy required was more concentrated and focused in a different way. It's worthwhile remembering that while there are such differences in the tone, feeling and content of a musical and a straight play, the essence of what you're doing – inhabiting a character, telling a story, engaging an audience – is the same for any type of theatre, and calls on every aspect of your professional attention.

## Television

Television is another pathway for many musical-theatre performers – and an important one in terms of exposure. Considering the enormous success of West End and Broadway shows, as well as the numerous touring productions at any one time, it does seem curious that television has not fully jumped on the bandwagon of musical theatre's popularity. Andrew Lloyd Webber's casting shows on the BBC (and, more recently, ITV) have been warmly received, and brought musicals to a primetime audience. Many performers already with very successful West End careers auditioned for *Superstar*, Lloyd Webber's 2012 televised mission to find Jesus, because they were aware how valuable the exposure to a much wider audience could be in terms of their overall careers. So perhaps the tide is turning.

If you are offered acting jobs on television, you will need to grasp them. Television is obviously a very different medium to theatre, but immensely valuable in developing new skills and your profile. In particular, the subtlety and realism required to perform on screen can only enhance your talents. Many stage actors initially struggle with the fact that television is almost never shot in the order in which the action takes place in the final product. In almost all instances, shooting takes place in fits and starts and from multiple angles.

In a BBC courtroom series called *The Case*, I filmed scenes for several different episodes all on the same day and in the same location, so that the film company could best utilise their limited time and finite space. Money is always a motivating factor in making these decisions, but the production teams are geniuses at piecing all the disparate parts together to make a coherent and dramatic episode or series. From an actor's point of view, it's worthwhile making notes that chart your character's thoughts, intentions and feelings for each scene you appear in. Then, if you're required to jump from filming Episode 1, Scene 17 straight to Episode 5, Scene 4, you can check your notes and see your character's thoughts at that moment. Personally, I always learn my lines in advance because it gives more time to develop the role before the shoot begins. That way I can focus on the character during the interminable breaks on set, rather than hurriedly learning lines.

You may get invited to appear as a guest, panellist or judge on various television shows. These can be great fun to do and some are fairly lucrative – but they often mean very long days. When I worked on a charity special of *Cash in the Attic*, it required two full days, from early in the morning till late at night, to get everything filmed – and that was for a thirty-minute programme. Another challenge is that you will rarely have the luxury of a long pre-shoot conversation with the director, or even the opportunity to rehearse with other actors. You get told, hurriedly, how the director envisages a shot being framed or a scene being filmed, but the responsibility to find your character will often fall solely on you.

Television and theatre both have their own idiosyncratic methods and madnesses and, hopefully, you'll have opportunities throughout your career to become intimately acquainted with all the quirks and unique characteristics of both of them.

### Working Overseas

Performing on Broadway is a dream for many actors, and can be a truly unforgettable, inspiring time. No doubt many American performers have the same feeling if they get the chance to appear in the West End. Working methods, audiences and living in the two transatlantic cities are very different; the Broadway audiences are very discerning, love their theatre, and are more enthused to take part in the whole experience. It's rare to see a show *not* received with a standing ovation, as opposed to London where it's something that happens occasionally.

Some successful West End productions transfer directly to Broadway (and vice versa), with the entire cast and creative team recreating the production. If you're lucky enough to be in one of these shows, it is the easiest, quickest and most secure way to end up performing on the other side of the Atlantic. The producer will be able to secure your visa to work, the arrangements will be made with Actors' Equity, and the show will hopefully repeat the success it must have achieved in its hometown to guarantee the transfer in the first place.

If you endeavour to work overseas as a freelance individual, obtaining a visa or green card is not easy. The application process is complicated and full of red tape, and is best done through a lawyer with extensive experience in immigration. Hailing from a different place and having a different sort of training, a different approach, and a different accent, can be the things that set you apart from the crowd – and that you can offer to a production. Always bear in mind that the grass is not necessarily greener on the other side of the pond. The reality of living and working permanently in a new country can be very different from what you expected, so make sure that you know what you're getting into and have spent sufficient time in your new city before you commit to the move.

## Fame

The day will come when everybody is famous for fifteen minutes, Andy Warhol once remarked. But long before Warhol was a spark in his father's eye, W.S. Gilbert (of the Gilbert and Sullivan partnership) had pointed out the more accurate opposite. He wrote in song for *The Gondoliers* that 'When everyone is somebody, then no one's *anybody*!'

Fame, of course, remains the spur for many, but musical theatre doesn't throw up big star names in quite the way it once did. The business is full of wonderful, well-trained performers who have paid their dues, learned their trade, and who, in the heyday of the old-fashioned musical, would indeed have been very famous. Times have changed. It is now pop singers, with their extreme television exposure, finding that kind of fame more or less instantly, whilst earning the sort of money that lots of top theatre talents will not make in a lifetime. Pop stars can deal in millions; the rest of us, sadly, live in the real world. It's tough, but that's the way it is. As the saying goes, if you can't cope, you shouldn't have joined.

The real truth is that young people come into musical theatre for the love of it. For most of them it is their *raison d'être*, and nothing is going to stop them trying to make it to the top. I am constantly amazed at the extraordinary range of talent out there. I can feel their passion and excitement. I share their hopes, and find myself looking forward to seeing their names up in lights.

Fame brings the odd perk. You may be offered future jobs without auditioning, you can always get a table at the restaurant of your choice, and it's sometimes nice to be recognised in the street. Getting your name at the top of the poster and your picture outside the theatre brings responsibilities. Lots of your spare time will be given over to publicising the show – photo-shoots, TV and radio interviews, newspaper features – and, as the star, you simply can't be ill. This was something I was used to because my parents were very strict and I only got a day off school if I was at death's door. In one show, I spent the whole performance either onstage or being sick in buckets in the wings. I don't think the audience noticed, but the cast certainly did.

With fame comes the fans. Musical-theatre fans and aficionados are generally nicer and less hysterical than they seem to be with film and TV personalities. They are enthusiastic but polite, and have a genuine interest in everything you do, without being too pushy. They are extremely loyal – and, of course, have a great taste in music!

Some can be fiercely faithful and devoted to particular shows. There's a lady in New York who has my face tattooed on her leg; while I was in *Chicago* on Broadway there was an elderly couple who attended every single matinee. Similarly, when I was in *Les Misérables* in London there was a woman who came to all the matinee performances and, it was said, had been doing so ever since the show started. It is quite remarkable that a number of fans will turn up wherever you happen to be performing, sometimes travelling the length and breadth of the country to find you. They love to chat and I have had nothing but kindness from them over many years. It's important to make time for them and show that kindness back, as often they are the unseen power plant behind your career.

## Not Working

Very few people in our business work, as it were, 'full time'. For the majority, there will be periods of unemployment in the industry, and we have had to earn a crust in some other fashion. Most performers in the theatre have, at some time or another, waited on tables or served behind a bar. It can be disappointing, but it keeps one kind of wolf from the door. Looked at in an optimistic way, it's all grist to the actor's mill.

We all need money, so it is sensible and in no way defeatist to have a back-up plan in mind; something that will hopefully keep you solvent and sane whilst allowing the freedom to attend meetings and auditions. I have a friend, a good-looking, accomplished actress, who did this for years until, finally, when the gaps between jobs got wider and wider, she drifted into teaching drama. But she'd be back onstage tomorrow if any kind of regular work was there for her. The old urge never goes away.

The clearer you can work out what it is you have got to do, and the better you plan, then the more you reduce the stress in your life, and the greater the chances are that you will succeed. It won't necessarily be because you are the best performer, but because so few people actually take the time and effort required to do this. It makes a lot of sense to have a personal strategy that does not leave everything to chance (or your agent).

## Staying Employed

It's been said that the reputation of a lifetime can often rest upon the conduct of a single moment. The theatre business is small and quite insular, and it makes sense to see that your standing in it stays good.

It's partly about how well you sing, dance and act, but also about your qualities as a person to work with. Many producers and creative teams will ask previous employers about the people to whom they consider offering a job, and casting directors will make it their business to find out what you're like in the rehearsal room and backstage as well as in performance.

It's a good thing to acknowledge that your reputation is an invaluable asset and can be one of the most compelling attributes in your career. Producers and directors want to work with people they can trust, so if you are difficult to work with, awkward, unfriendly, bullying, unprofessional, argumentative – even if just the once – then there comes a point when any talent is outweighed by that reputation. And then it can be curtains for your career.

# Finale

Performing in musical theatre is always an exhilarating, exacting, infinitely rewarding experience. Every stage you tread upon and every theatre family you become part of will remain warmly, indelibly in your memory. We are so fortunate to have our greatest passion as our occupation. Wherever your journey takes you, we sincerely hope that you will be blessed with as much happiness and joy as musical theatre has brought us.

# Appendices

# Training in the UK

Drama UK is the organisation (replacing the Conference of Drama Schools and the National Council for Drama Training) that offers advice on professional training in the UK. Their incredibly useful guide to all the available accredited courses can be downloaded from their website: www.dramauk.co.uk

Member schools of Drama UK offer vocational courses for students over the age of eighteen. All schools offer a three-year full-time acting course (diploma or degree), or one-year full-time postgraduate courses (diploma or MA). The members offering courses in performance are listed here, and those with a specialist musical-theatre training appear in bold, with a list of their musical-theatre courses. Those institutions offering part-time or short courses in musical theatre (sometimes as short as a week) have an asterisk (*) after their name; see each institution's website for more details on these.

Academy of Live and Recorded Arts, London
www.alra.co.uk

**ArtsEd (Arts Educational Schools)**, London*
www.artsed.co.uk
*Foundation (1yr), Diploma (3yr), BA (3yr), MA in Creative Practice (1yr)*

BSA (Birmingham School of Acting)*
www.bcu.ac.uk/bsa

Bristol Old Vic Theatre School
www.oldvic.ac.uk

**Central School of Speech and Drama**, London\*
www.cssd.ac.uk
*BA (3yr), MA in Music Theatre (1yr)*

Cygnet Training Theatre, Exeter, Devon
www.cygnetnewtheatre.com

Drama Centre London
www.csm.arts.ac.uk/drama

Drama Studio London
www.dramastudiolondon.co.uk

East 15 Acting School, London
www.east15.ac.uk

**GSA (Guildford School of Acting)**, Surrey\*
www.gsauk.org
*Foundation (1yr), Diploma (3yr), BA (3yr), MA in Musical Theatre (1yr)*

Guildhall School of Music & Drama, London\*
www.gsmd.ac.uk

Italia Conti Academy of Theatre Arts, London
www.italiaconti-acting.co.uk

LAMDA (London Academy of Music and Dramatic Art)\*
www.lamda.org.uk

LIPA (Liverpool Institute for Performing Arts)\*
www.lipa.ac.uk

MMU (Manchester Metropolitan University School of Theatre)
www.theatre.mmu.ac.uk

**Mountview Academy of Theatre Arts,** London*
www.mountview.org.uk
*Foundation (1yr), Diploma (3yr), BA (3yr), MA/PG Dip in Performance (1yr)*

**The Oxford School of Drama**
www.oxforddrama.ac.uk
*Foundation (6 months)*

RADA (Royal Academy of Dramatic Art), London*
www.rada.ac.uk

Rose Bruford College of Theatre & Performance, Sidcup, Kent
www.bruford.ac.uk

**Royal Conservatoire of Scotland,** Glasgow*
www.rcs.ac.uk
*BA (3yr), MA (1yr)*

**RWCMD (Royal Welsh College of Music & Drama),** Cardiff
www.rwcmd.ac.uk
*MA (1yr)*

The following schools and colleges, which may lean slightly more towards dance, includes those that are accredited but are not in the core Drama UK member institutions. They all offer different diplomas and courses in musical theatre; check their websites for details:

Bird College, Sidcup, Kent
www.birdcollege.co.uk

Bodywork Dance Studio, Cambridge
www.bodywork-dance.co.uk

CPA Studios (Colin's Performing Arts), Romford, Essex
www.cpastudios.co.uk

Expressions Academy of Performing Arts, Mansfield, Notts
www.expressionsperformingarts.co.uk

Laine Theatre Arts, Epsom, Surrey
www.laine-theatre-arts.co.uk

Liverpool Theatre School and College
www.liverpooltheatreschoolandcollege.co.uk

Midlands Academy of Dance and Drama, Nottingham
www.maddcollege.co.uk

Millennium Dance 2000, London
www.md2000.co.uk

Performers College, Corringham, Essex
www.performerscollege.co.uk

Royal Academy of Music, London
www.ram.ac.uk

Stella Mann College, Bedford
www.stellamanncollege.co.uk

Urdang Academy, London
www.theurdangacademy.com

The following schools and colleges also offer musical-theatre
training (sometimes specialising in dance):

American Musical Theatre Academy, London
www.americanacademy.co.uk

Amersham and Wycombe College, Chesham, Bucks
www.amersham.ac.uk

Blackpool and The Fylde College, Lancashire
www.blackpool.ac.uk

Bournemouth and Poole College, Dorset
www.thecollege.co.uk

City Lit, London
www.citylit.ac.uk

D&B School of Performing Arts, Bromley, Kent
www.dandbperformingarts.co.uk

Elmhurst School for Dance, Birmingham
www.elmhurstdance.co.uk

English National Ballet School, London
www.enbschool.org.uk

Glasgow Academy Musical Theatre Arts
www.gamta.org.uk

Hammond School, Chester, Cheshire
www.thehammondschool.co.uk

KSA Performing Arts (Kent Stage Academy), Beckenham,
Kent
www.ksapa.co.uk

London School of Musical Theatre
www.lsmt.co.uk

London Studio Centre
www.london-studio-centre.co.uk

London Theatre School
www.londontheatreschool.co.uk

Merseyside Dance and Drama Centre, Liverpool
www.mddcdance.co.uk

MGA Academy of Performing Arts, Edinburgh
www.themgaacademy.com

Musical Theatre Academy, London
www.themta.co.uk

Music Theatre Scotland, Newcastleton, Roxburghshire
www.musictheatrescotland.co.uk

Northern Ballet School, Manchester
www.northernballetschool.co.uk

PPA (Performance Preparation Academy), Guildford,
Surrey
www.ppacademy.co.uk

Read Dance and Theatre College, Reading, Berkshire
www.rdtc.org.uk

Reynolds Performing Arts Academy, Bexley, Kent
www.reynoldsgroup.co.uk

SLP College, Leeds
www.slpcollege.co.uk

Tring Park School for the Performing Arts, Herts
www.tringpark.com

WAC Performing Arts and Media College
www.wac.co.uk


The following schools and organisations offer musical-
theatre training for children and young people (both
full-time and part-time); check online for details:

Arabesque School for Performing Arts, Chichester,
West Sussex

Barbara Speake Stage School, London

Brit School for Performing Arts and Technology, Croydon

CPA Studios (Colin's Performing Arts), Romford, Essex

Italia Conti Academy of Theatre Arts, London

LIPA 4:19, UK-wide franchise

National Youth Theatre, London

National Youth Music Theatre, London

Paul Nicholas School of Acting and Performing Arts, UK-wide franchise

Pauline Quirke Academy of Performing Arts, UK-wide franchise

PPA, Guildford, Surrey

Razzamataz, UK-wide franchise

Redroofs Theatre School, Maidenhead, Berks

Reynolds Training Academy, Dartford, Kent

Royal Conservatoire of Scotland

Stagecoach Theatre Arts Schools, UK-wide franchise

Susi Earnshaw Theatre School, Barnet, Herts

Sylvia Young Theatre School, London

Theatretrain, UK-wide franchise

West End Kids, Rochester, Kent

West End Stage School, London

Youth Music Theatre UK, London

# Useful Websites

*Training*

CDET (Council for Dance Education and Training)
www.cdet.org.uk

Drama UK    www.dramauk.co.uk

Masterclass    www.masterclass.org.uk


*Youth Theatres*

National Association of Youth Theatres    www.nayt.org.uk

National Youth Music Theatre    www.nymt.org.uk

National Youth Theatre    www.nyt.org.uk

Youth Dance England    www.yde.org.uk

Youth Music Theatre UK    www.youthmusictheatreuk.org


*Amateur Theatre*

Amateur Theatre Network    www.amdram.co.uk

Little Theatre Guild    www.littletheatreguild.org

National Operatic and Dramatic Association
www.noda.org.uk

National Drama Festivals Association    www.ndfa.org.uk

*Coaches*

Association of Teachers of Singing    www.aotos.co.uk

International Dance Teachers Association
www.idta.co.uk

Music Teachers    www.musicteachers.co.uk

Vocal Tutors    www.vocaltutors.co.uk


*Professional Organisations*

Casting Call Pro    www.castingcallpro.com

Equity    www.equity.org.uk

Production and Casting Report (PCR)
www.pcrnewsletter.com

Spotlight    www.spotlight.com

*The Stage* newspaper    www.thestage.co.uk


*Theatre News and Gossip*

Broadway.com    www.broadway.com

Broadway World    www.broadwayworld.com

London Theatre Guide Online    www.londontheatre.co.uk

Official London Theatre
www.officiallondontheatre.co.uk

What'sOnStage.com    www.whatsonstage.com